T0090584

THE PSYCHOLOGY OF TRAUMA

What emotional, physical, and psychological effects might there be on those who have experienced traumatic events? How does neurodiversity, culture, and individual experience affect trauma responses? How can you support someone experiencing symptoms of trauma?

The Psychology of Trauma integrates the knowledge and research from clinical practice and neuroscience to offer a scientific approach to understanding and managing symptoms of trauma. It debunks the myths and prejudices around trauma-informed therapy, shifting people's view from 'What's wrong with you?' to 'What happened to you?', and provides an overview of the different concepts and counselling approaches that are most suitable to support working with trauma. It also explores how neurodiversity, cultural differences, or social contexts affect the way we respond to any trauma.

Using a trauma-informed framework, The Psychology of Trauma explores how clinical understanding can help family and community to support the journey of recovery. It provides an overview of key aspects around trauma-informed practices and principles whilst shining a light on new and emerging treatments for trauma.

Dr Shanti Farrington is a Chartered Psychologist (BPS) and trained as an integrative counsellor and a registered member of the British Association for Counselling and Psychotherapy (UK). Shanti works as Principal Academic (Psychology) with Bournemouth University and is Honorary Associate Psychologist, Acquired Brain Injury and Rehabilitation Services, Dorset HealthCare University Foundation Trust. She is the cofounder of Sheetal Astitva – a charity (Pune, India) and The Trauma-Informed Practice Services, a community interest company (CIC) developed to offer low-cost therapy and accessible training for people affected by, or working with, trauma. She has previously worked as a counsellor within sexual trauma organisations.

Alison Woodward trained as a United Kingdom Council for Psychotherapy–accredited psychotherapist and Certified Transactional Analyst (CTA) at The Metanoia Institute, London, and currently works in her private practice and as a senior lecturer at Bournemouth University. She is the cofounder of The Trauma-Informed Practice Services, a CIC developed to offer low-cost therapy and accessible training for people affected by, or working with, trauma. She has previously worked within sexual trauma organisations, jointly leading the provision of clinical therapeutic services.

THE PSYCHOLOGY OF EVERYTHING

People are fascinated by psychology, and what makes humans tick. Why do we think and behave the way we do? We've all met armchair psychologists claiming to have the answers, and people that ask if psychologists can tell what they're thinking. The Psychology of Everything is a series of books which debunk the popular myths and pseudo-science surrounding some of life's biggest questions.

The series explores the hidden psychological factors that drive us, from our subconscious desires and aversions to our natural social instincts. Absorbing, informative, and always intriguing, each book is written by an expert in the field, examining how research-based knowledge compares with popular wisdom, and showing how psychology can truly enrich our understanding of modern life.

Applying a psychological lens to an array of topics and contemporary concerns – from sex, to fashion, to conspiracy theories – The Psychology of Everything will make you look at everything in a new way.

Titles in the series:

For more information about this series, please visit: www.routledgetextbooks.com/textbooks/thepsychologyofeverything/

THE PSYCHOLOGY OF TRAUMA

OF TRAUMA

DR SHANTI FARRINGTON AND ALISON WOODWARD

Routledge
Taylor & Francis Group

LONDON AND NEW YORK

First published 2025
by Routledge
4 Park Square, Milton Park, Abingdon, Oxon OX14 4RN

and by Routledge
605 Third Avenue, New York, NY 10158

Routledge is an imprint of the Taylor & Francis Group, an informa business

British Library Cataloguing-in-Publication Data
A catalogue record for this book is available from the British Library

ISBN: 978-1-032-63723-5 (hbk)
ISBN: 978-1-032-63722-8 (pbk)
ISBN: 978-1-032-63724-2 (ebk)

DOI: 10.4324/9781032637242

Typeset in Joanna
by Apex CoVantage, LLC

We would like to thank all our clients who have trusted us and taught us with humility how to be in the moment and be present to trauma. We would like to honour the courage they had to engage in the process and grow their experience.

CONTENTS

PREFACE

In everyday life often we experience events that are distressing and use the term, *'that was traumatic'*. You perhaps have picked up this book because of something you have experienced or witnessed and are interested in understanding more about the impact of trauma on our lives. This book provides a brief overview of the emotional, physical, and psychological effects of experiencing traumatic events. It is ideal for someone who wants to understand the psychology of trauma and can help you decide if you need more support from professionals (like counsellors, psychotherapists, or psychologists) to support your well-being.

It will also be useful for students and qualified practitioners who want more knowledge of trauma-informed psychotherapy and what the differences are to our core training, whilst simultaneously giving an overview about the trauma-informed approach to those who are not in this as a profession. Some parts of this book may provide a quick overview of certain aspects of trauma-informed counselling, while other chapters expand on knowledge and bring together aspects of the impact of trauma from a global perspective. Finally, a section addresses the common myths and assumptions that can be present with both individuals and society.

ACKNOWLEDGEMENT

The authors would like to thank Gerry Jones and Dr. Gizem Arabaci for their mentorship, experience, and continued support and for taking the time to read and give us insightful and valuable comments on the first draft.

Our families have been an invaluable source of support throughout the process, and we thank Sam, Charlotte, and Bethan Woodward and Jon Farrington for their patience and love.

INTRODUCTION

Experiences that are beyond the individual's control and cause physical, psychological, or emotional distress in a person, affecting their coping ability, are referred to as 'trauma'. Trauma can affect the person's emotional, physical, social, or psychological well-being, either for a short period or, in some cases, may have long-lasting effects. Understanding how the human survival instinct impacts our body systems, alongside our early life experiences and attachments, is key to processing our experience(s) and helping the individual to cope with the traumatic experience.

Experience of a traumatic event does not always result in post-traumatic stress disorder (PTSD), though individuals may experience one or more symptoms immediately after the event, known as acute stress disorder (APA, 2013). With good support and a space to process these experiences, these symptoms usually reduce over time. A diagnosis of PTSD is made by medical professionals, if these symptoms persist for one or more months (APA, 2013). When someone experiences a series of repeated traumatic events from an early age, it is referred to as complex trauma (CPTSD). The impact of the trauma symptoms in CPTSD are usually more enduring and normally require long-term professional support for the person to be able to process and recover over time.

DOI: 10.4324/9781032637242-1

The *Psychology of Trauma* aims to consolidate the current understanding around PTSD/CPTSD. Understanding the psychology of trauma will not only support individuals to be empowered to manage their trauma symptoms effectively, but also encourage them to engage with appropriate support through counselling or psychotherapy. Knowledge from neuroscience and research is integrated with a practical and clinical understanding of trauma. This book combines the academic perspectives with everyday issues from a therapeutic point of view, whilst highlighting the impact counselling can have on mental well-being. It aims to debunk the myths and prejudices around trauma-informed therapy, shifting from a 'What's wrong with you?' to a 'What happened to you?' perspective. It provides an overview of the trauma-informed approach to psychotherapy and counselling in an easy-to-read format.

The book explores how neurodiversity and cultural differences affect the way individuals respond to any trauma. Breaking common myths and the rigid thoughts around trauma, it ties together the role of online counselling and the importance of one-on-one face-to-face sessions. It discusses how a trauma-informed approach in psychotherapy is critical to managing everyday issues, and considers the adaptations needed to make it effective for people living with different psychological or neurological disorders. The book uses a framework that integrates evidence-based therapeutic or clinical work in a trauma-informed approach whilst also bringing in the role of family and community in supporting this journey.

As part of the *Psychology of Everything* series, this book is aimed at people who may be interested to learn more about trauma, including professionals (e.g., clinicians, counsellors, psychologists, or academics). Overall, it offers a concise and engaging narrative to empower readers to begin to ask questions about 'What has happened to me/you?' and to be curious about the impact of trauma.

Good enough is what is as close to perfect as one can get!

1

WHAT IS TRAUMA?

THE EVER-CHANGING LANDSCAPE OF TRAUMA

Take a moment to reflect as you begin to read this book. Whenever you hear the word 'trauma', what comes to your mind? It's normally war, or an accident that may be catastrophic. How many of us also think about our everyday experiences, like how we are treated at work by others, our employers, or in our relationships, as being traumatic? The word 'trauma' is commonly used, but do we stop to consider how our past experiences impact our responses and therefore our everyday lives?

It can therefore be expected that individuals will have slightly different definitions of trauma; some may focus on the physical nature (i.e., an accident or medical incident), others on big disasters or world events, and some more on the psychological impact of relationships. The truth is that trauma is all of these things and more. Our world history is littered with significant traumas, world wars, natural disasters, pandemics, genocide, and political crisis, the aftermath of which impact both the individual who experiences it and their future generations. Most recently the climate change agenda, the aftermath of a global pandemic, and an economic crisis continue to perpetuate a sense of traumatic experiences. Our response to these can define how we relate to people and how we feel about ourselves, yet 'how' we have responded is often thought about with judgement and

DOI: 10.4324/9781032637242-2

prejudice – with expectations that we 'should' respond in a certain way or 'be over it already'. This makes navigating the impact of trauma extremely tricky and shaming for those who are in the middle of it.

This book was conceptualised to help reduce the stigma by normalising the psychological and other symptoms that can manifest while recognising the possibility of post-traumatic growth (Sanderson, 2013). It aims to offer a wealth of psychoeducation to explain the biological, neurological, and other factors that happen automatically in our brains and bodies when we feel threatened, with a view to shifting perception from "I am bad/unable to manage/ crazy, etc." to one of "I survived something terrible and now I am managing the best I can, dealing with the symptoms as best as I can".

In this first chapter we define what trauma is (and isn't) and introduce the wider concepts that are expanded as we move through the book. Our experiences of working with people from diverse backgrounds are shared, with a particular view to encouraging curiosity within ourselves about our responses, and our thoughts when we encounter people who have experienced trauma. We argue that many life experiences can be viewed as traumatic, while also challenging the societal beliefs about people who might have relational difficulties after living through and surviving their experience. We invite you to challenge your own views as you read – for example, what is it you might have thought about someone's behaviour that potentially alienates or discounts the experiences they may have had, and how that means trusting or relating to you might feel terrifying?

Trauma is such a broad term, so let's look to a commonly used definition to help us refine what we mean:

> Trauma is an emotional response to a terrible event like an accident, rape, or natural disaster.
>
> (*APA*, 2023)

This definition by the American Psychological Association (APA) encapsulates the breadth of the impact of trauma; no two people who experience the same traumatic event will have the same presentation of responses – this is something that is exceedingly difficult to keep in mind in the aftermath of the trauma. For example, when a natural disaster occurs survivors often report feeling 'guilty' that they have not been as psychologically impacted as others. The concept of survivor's guilt (Niederland, 1968) is well documented, and we see it here at the start of our journey being an important part of our own judgement as to how well (or not) we cope with the difficult things life throws at us.

> Immediately after the event, shock and denial are typical. Longer term reactions include unpredictable emotions, flashbacks, strained relationships, and even physical symptoms like headaches or nausea.
>
> (*APA, accessed* 2023)

This additional aspect of the APA's definition starts to suggest the range of emotional and physical symptoms that can be present when trauma has been experienced, and how complex these phenomena are. The UK government (Nov, 2023) defined trauma as follows:

> Trauma results from an event, series of events, or set of circumstances that is experienced by an individual as harmful or life threatening. While unique to the individual, generally the experience of trauma can cause lasting adverse effects, limiting the ability to function and achieve mental, physical, social, emotional, or spiritual well-being.
>
> (www.gov.uk, 2023)

A common misconception is that when we experience something difficult, we should move on quickly, and are expected to cope and function without any consequence. For example, if we happened to be in a car accident that isn't terribly serious, perhaps a minor bump from a car behind us, where we experienced a small physical whiplash injury from the seatbelt and a small cut from the airbag deploying, we would probably be encouraged to: "get straight back in the car, carry on driving – it's the best way". These 'get on with it' messages from self or society often create a shaming response. If we are still impacted, when we get behind the wheel, it's natural to feel anxious, perhaps even have a panic attack; the expectations to carry on prevent us from sharing the impact, and we may cry when we are alone, trying our best to ignore or mask the symptoms. Throughout this book we will explore various aspects of trauma keeping in mind neurodiversity, culture, and familial relationships whilst building a picture of the complexity of relational patterns underlying trauma.

The terms counselling or psychotherapy may sometimes be used interchangeably within this book; however, in practise counselling is normally briefer and goal orientated to address any current or ongoing issues, whereas psychotherapy will do the same but may also address the reasons that may contribute to the development of the current problems. Psychotherapy tends to be more long term and relational in its approach. In either of these the client can choose to take a break and come back. There is plenty of evidence (McLean & Foa, 2011; Lely et al., 2019) to suggest that exposure therapies (narrative and prolonged approaches) are the right way to manage traumatic experiences; cognitive behavioural therapists would potentially set 'exposure' or 'confrontation' as a homework task for a client (Foa et al., 2008) to understand that the risk has passed, and they are safe now. This approach may be successful for some, particularly if the car accident in our example wasn't life threatening and more importantly, if we have not experienced any previous trauma in which our brain has recognised that we are 'not safe'.

The difficulty comes when the one-off car accident (in this example) is not the first trauma, or if this first accident is very severe and has caused significant impact physically. This event could bring into awareness some of the past minor relational transgressions, traumas, and life experiences. How our brains respond to this seemingly one-off event will vary. In some people the response may seem out of proportion and overexaggerated. This is because, although we are consciously dealing with the current traumatic experiences, our brain has linked it automatically to our past struggles and trauma (Levine,

2015). Although we may cognitively know that we are dealing with the present car accident, our brain is unable to differentiate this from the past personal struggles, relationship breakdown, or the abusive parent or partner, chronic illness, or cultural breach already experienced, and responds dramatically to this event. For example, the bang of the crash might remind our brains of the bang of the doors being slammed when we were younger when parents were arguing, or of being jumped on in school, by bullies. The jolt of the seatbelt might reactivate an old sporting injury or perhaps remind us of when we were assaulted by a parent or partner earlier in our lives. None of these connections will be made in our conscious thought but explicitly felt in our bodies, meaning our response is layered with our previous experiences.

Over the past decade, empirical research has been supporting Freud's (1915/57) concept of repression. Specifically, we are aware that our brain actively suppresses unwanted memories and that survival is the key to this suppression or repression. We will discuss more about this in Chapter 2 (where we discuss the neuroscience of trauma). To help understand this common yet complex response further, we will first look at the wider definitions of terms used when discussing trauma, and how it may be linked to secondary trauma (vicarious trauma).

POST-TRAUMATIC STRESS DISORDER (PTSD)

PTSD was first noticed and treated as a psychological disorder following the First World War. It was reported that soldiers were experiencing 'shell shock' (Myers, 1915) as a direct result of the things they had seen and been ordered to do in the trenches of France. Over the following years most research related to PTSD was linked to returning soldiers and veterans of war, noticing the reoccurring and debilitating aspects of the psychological distress they were experiencing (Belenky, 1987).

The *Diagnostic and Statistical Manual of Mental Disorders*, Fifth Edition (DSM-V,[1] APA, 2013) focuses on the behavioural aspects of the response to trauma and centres on four key clusters – re-experiencing, avoidance, negative cognitions and mood, and arousal – to diagnose PTSD (see Appendix for full diagnostic criteria). In addition to having the symptoms listed in the DSM-V criteria, they have to be causing significant distress or impairment in social, occupational, or other important areas of functioning, and they cannot be attributed to any other physiological effect of a substance (e.g., medication or alcohol) or another medical condition, and present for at least one month or more (anything less could be considered acute stress disorder, APA, 2013, pp. 271–272).[2]

COMPLEX POST-TRAUMATIC STRESS DISORDER (CPTSD)

A PTSD diagnosis sometimes does not seem to capture the chronic nature and often inherent behavioural responses displayed by people who have experienced repeated trauma from a young age. These responses are often misinterpreted as 'personality' or people being 'difficult', 'reactive', or having a diagnosis of unhelpful conditions such as personality disorders (Orcutt, 2012). The International Classification of Diseases – Version 11 (ICD-11), recognised by the World Health Organisation (2018), is the alternative psychiatric diagnostic manual to the DSM-V. The ICD-11 does recognise an additional condition closely linked to PTSD but specified for when abuse, neglect, or relational attachments have been disrupted early in childhood. Complex PTSD is a condition which is becoming more widely recognised; it has the same core aspects of PTSD but with three additional components. Examples of presentation may include: 1) problems in affect regulation (such as marked irritability or anger, feeling emotionally numb); 2) beliefs about oneself as diminished, defeated, or worthless, accompanied by feelings of shame, guilt, or failure related to the traumatic event; 3) difficulties in sustaining relationships and in feeling close to others (UK Trauma Council, accessed 2023).

WHAT HAPPENS WHEN YOU WITNESS OR HEAR ABOUT TRAUMA?

Another difficult preconception about the impact of trauma is one where if you haven't experienced it you 'shouldn't' be impacted by it; this also can be true of grief or loss. Reflect for a moment, how many times have you said to yourself or a trusted other, "but it didn't happen to me, why is it affecting me?" As a society we can consider experiencing trauma as more significant than witnessing it, yet the impact is often as debilitating (Sheen et al., 2014). There are, of course, differences – when we directly experience trauma there may be physical injuries, emotional distress, and a somatic sense of what happened to us may be held as tension or stress in our body.

SECONDARY TRAUMA OR VICARIOUS TRAUMA

Secondary trauma is the term that can be used when we are impacted indirectly by someone else's trauma. Often called various trauma ('vicarious' is derived from Latin – meaning 'substituted' and 'trauma' is derived from Greek – meaning 'wound') we can find ourselves experiencing symptoms of trauma even when we haven't been involved in the other's traumatic experience. For example, people who work in a professional capacity supporting those in crisis (e.g., mental health teams, charities, medicine, psychological support work, schools, etc.) can find themselves feeling increasingly anxious about things that haven't happened to them; they might have nightmares, sleep disturbances, and other traumatic symptoms. Vicarious trauma can be linked to the development of compassion fatigue, burn-out, the cost of caring, and the impact is as significant as directly experiencing the trauma itself.

SINGLE-EVENT AND RELATIONAL OR COMPLEX TRAUMA

Medical diagnosis is useful for several reasons and provides access to services for psychological support (in some countries). Diagnosis can give reassurance that what someone is experiencing is 'normal' and to be expected, but it can also bring stigma, shame, and resistance to change. This book holds medical diagnosis as a vital part of an individual's journey to recovery and it recognises that thinking psychotherapeutically about what someone is experiencing is also important. So here, in an imagined case study, we offer a relational explanation of the diagnostic criteria found in the DSM-V or ICD-11.

Example 1:

Imagine for a moment a loving couple (gender or sexuality of your choice). This couple decides to start a family and either by natural means (i.e., heterosexual couple having sex and conceiving a child) or by supported conception (i.e., IVF/surrogacy/adoption, etc.), this couple brings a child into their family unit and provides good enough care supporting them through the early years of that child's life.

As the child grows up difficult things happen. They experience bullying at school, one of the parents has a cancer diagnosis, which means that for a period a primary carer is less available to them. As they reach adulthood the parent who has been ill for several years dies, leaving one parent to grieve with them. How do you think the child will manage those difficult traumas?

Example 2:

A young teenage girl gets pregnant within a relationship; the father is older and not interested in the mother as her pregnancy progresses. The child is born, and the mother has long periods of post-natal depression. She parents the child as well as she can, but the second parental figure is absent and when discussed is painted as 'not good'.

The mother has a series of abusive (physically and sexually) relationships and the child's emotional needs are missed. The situation in the house is chaotic, and the child is vulnerable to seeking unsafe attachments, resulting in multiple adults abusing the child physically or sexually. The child also experiences bullying at school and the mother has chronic health conditions, which means as the child moves towards adulthood, they have little adult support or guidance.

How do you think this second child might manage these difficult traumas?

Example 3:

A young adult (identifies as gay) has generally coped well with life, has no history of sexual or physical abuse as a child, and is coping well with life. He is still in his 30s, does keep in touch with his mother, and has some good friends. He has had some interim relationships but nothing very serious. He has had two assaults in the past, based on homophobic reactions to him. This external event has caused him to experience PTSD, and he is now not in any romantic relationship and is struggling to cope in everyday life.

Now imagine how this example may be different from the two other examples. This is an example of how there may not necessarily be a past abuse or developmental issues, but the individual has in adulthood been exposed to an event of assault, that has triggered some of the fears of his identity and insecure attachment, which can be resolved through counselling.

The purpose of outlining these three distinctly different circumstances is to illustrate that the foundations of our childhood directly influence how we choose to respond to stimulus as we grow up. The child that has secure foundations will still experience difficulties and traumatic events but will be better equipped to process and manage these traumas and develop relationships with trusted adults and professionals. The child that did not have security in their early life will be more likely to have developed coping strategies that are deemed in society as 'difficult' or 'wrong'. Whilst the strategies may be maladaptive, they probably ensured that as a child their needs were partially met or met as best they could be; this was their normal. This is derived from attachment theory, first researched and developed by Bowlby in the late 1950s and early 1960s. This thinking that attachment styles from childhood affect trauma responses now forms the basis of complex PTSD and relational trauma diagnoses (Fisher, 2017).

An analogy of a tower of stacked pennies (Berne, 1961) is useful to help understand the development of resilience through our early attachments. The 'bent penny' phenomenon is one explanation for the individual differences; it describes how we can all experience trauma, but if the initial building blocks are stable (i.e., the pennies are all level and intact), our systems (psychological and physiological) can sustain the trauma and recover. However, if the foundations are unsteady and all bent by multiple and repeated traumas then there is no stability, resulting in a precarious structure and potentially the risk of a full system collapse.

Transactional analysis suggests than when faced with adversity and in general we will approach a situation from one of four life positions (Ernst, 1971, see Figure 1.1).[3] Thinking from this perspective gives us a language to think about how we are feeling at any given time in relationship with the other, particularly when we are experiencing a traumatic situation. Depending on our past experiences of being

<table>
<tr><td rowspan="3">I am not Okay with me</td><td colspan="2">You are Okay with me</td><td rowspan="3">I am Okay with me</td></tr>
<tr><td>I am not OK, you are OK (one down position)

Response: Get away from helplessness (depressive position)</td><td>I am OK, you are OK (healthy position)

Response: Get on with, you are happy.</td></tr>
<tr><td>I am not OK; you are not OK. (hopeless position)

Response: get nowhere with, the feeling is of hopelessness.</td><td>I am OK, you are not OK (one up position)

Response: get rid of, feeling is angry.</td></tr>
<tr><td></td><td colspan="2">You are not Okay with me</td><td></td></tr>
</table>

Figure 1.1 The Okay Corral

Source: Adapted from Ernst (1971)

responded to, we will assume one of the four life positions. The lens that we view our world through will change depending on circumstances, when we think others are not 'okay' we can make assumptions as to whether we are safe in our environment. If we don't feel safe, or when we have experienced trauma, then our behaviour will automatically be defensive, as our brain is switching on the survival mechanism. This response is what is often viewed as 'difficult' or 'not okay' by others (see Chapter 2, Neuroscience of trauma).

TRAUMA FROM ACQUIRED EVENTS

Very often when we think of trauma from a counselling or psychological perspective, we default to the trauma that may be caused by physical, sexual, or emotional abuse. However, any event, such as natural disasters, accidents, falls, developing a medical condition, or losing someone, can also be traumatic. Initially, cognitive behavioural therapy (CBT) was the most often used intervention to support recovery; however, today there is evidence that other therapies beyond CBT are helpful, especially when dealing with complex trauma. Approaches to working with PTSD or complex trauma often use a more trauma-informed approach, including aspects from other therapeutic modalities, such as attachment therapy, internal family systems, somatic psychotherapy, and psychodynamic therapy. In this book we will integrate the trauma-informed framework to various therapeutic approaches to address the core issues.

SYMPTOMS OF TRAUMA

As we bring the introduction to an end it is worth noting the wide range and vast symptoms that can be linked to experiencing trauma. These symptoms show that the individual has endured and survived extreme circumstances that placed incredible stress on their physical body and nervous systems. The model (referred to here as the trauma cloud) presented in Figure 1.2, outlines some of the main symptoms that can be experienced, illustrating the complexity and individual

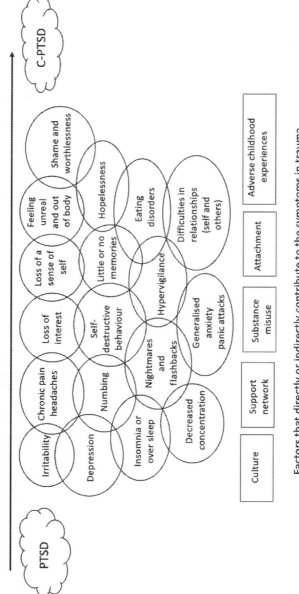

Low severity to high severity of manifestation of symptoms in relation to trauma

PTSD

C-PTSD

Irritability

Chronic pain headaches

Loss of interest

Loss of a sense of self

Feeling unreal and out of body

Shame and worthlessness

Depression

Numbing

Self-destructive behaviour

Little or no memories

Hopelessness

Insomnia or over sleep

Nightmares and flashbacks

Hypervigilance

Eating disorders

Decreased concentration

Generalised anxiety panic attacks

Difficulties in relationships (self and others)

Factors that directly or indirectly contribute to the symptoms in trauma

Culture

Support network

Substance misuse

Attachment

Adverse childhood experiences

Figure 1.2 The trauma cloud

differences in the presentation of trauma. It also shows how external factors contribute towards the shift of the presentation, moving from PTSD to C-PTSD.

Until relatively recently (c. 1980) psychological symptoms were not readily recognised in the general population; PTSD was associated mainly with veterans. Research has shifted the thinking to show that experiencing any difficult event can cause symptoms of trauma like the veterans experienced (Herman, 1992; Fisher, 2017, 2021; Van Der Kolk, 2014). Harvey (1996) stated:

> Trauma Survivors have symptoms not memories
>
> (Harvey, 1996)

As you read on through the chapters of this book, keep in mind our absolute philosophy regarding this statement. Notice how this might shift the perceptions of yourself and people you know as you begin to view the impact of trauma through this very different lens.

Ask not what is wrong with you, but what has happened to you?

THE FORMAT FOR CLINICAL CASE EXAMPLES USED IN THE BOOK

The Psychology of Trauma is intended to be an introduction and overview, not only to people who may be interested in or have experienced trauma, but also an easy read for professionals who work in areas of mental health or psychological support but may be interested in learning more about trauma. The case studies used in this book are either fictitious ones (to convey a point) or real case examples (clients have verbally or in writing consented for the use of the content) where the client will be anonymous, but the lessons learnt from the experience will be shared to help learn more with this real example. Any case examples in this book will be discussed with a focus towards what shifted in the client, and end with our own reflections on the process. The case examples discussed will use a trauma-informed approach integrating the core principles from different therapeutic modalities that have been efficient.

NOTES

1 One of the internationally recognised medical psychiatric diagnostic tools used by health professionals.
2 The criteria only apply to adults, adolescents, and children older than 6 years.
3 The four life positions described by transactional analysis are I'm OK – you're OK; I'm OK –you're not OK; I'm not OK – you're OK; I'm not OK – you are not OK.

2

NEUROSCIENCE OF TRAUMA

BASIC NEUROANATOMY

The human brain has evolved from our animal ancestors over millions of years and elements of how it operates in our world today are still the same. The frontal lobe is the most recent and 'human' part of the brain; this part that is more sophisticated in its process and is what differentiates us from animals as it allows us to think, plan, and solve problems. It is also the aspect that when we experience trauma, does not work as well (if at all), which means it is often difficult for us to understand and process what happened. One view of the evolution of the human brain comes from the model also known as the triune brain (MacLean, 1990). This model proposes that there are three main regions or sections of the brain: 1) the primitive brain (also referred to as the reptilian complex); 2) the limbic system (the paleomammalian complex); and 3) the new cortex (the neomammalian cortex).

Historically, the primitive brain is thought to kick in and overtake some of our conscious frontal lobe (the new cortex) functions, especially when there is a threat to survival – ultimately it is more important to stay alive than to think. The limbic system, also often referred to as the emotional network (or the papez circuit) in the brain, is composed of a number of subcortical structures and is not only evolutionarily geared to recognise threat, both internal and

DOI: 10.4324/9781032637242-3

external, but it also feeds into the learning and belief systems we develop based on the experience. This means it tries to anticipate future threats based on our past experiences, yet this is done without the correct here and now information, so it can get it wrong and assumes there is threat when we are actually safe. The new cortex or the frontal lobe is what we may call the human brain and includes the frontal region which is the key to higher cognitive functions such as language, planning, inhibiting responses or movements or thoughts, ability to think from an abstract perspective, etc.

When we think about our trauma responses it is the midbrain that is governing our thoughts, behaviour, and actions. We can think of this a higher-ranking officer on a covert operation with high stakes; they might see a life-threatening danger that no-one else has, and they swoop in to take control of the operation to prevent a disaster from happening. Our midbrain (or limbic system) does the same; it takes over to keep us alive when it feels there is a risk − it is the area that supports our intuitive response when faced with a threat from the environment or we sense an internal threat from ourselves. The midbrain (limbic system) is also sometimes referred to as the emotional brain and, when activated, because it fears there is a threat, it overrides the executive cortex functioning (which is the part that gives us our logical and the here and now sense of safety). Therefore, when faced with any threat, our limbic systems respond in the most suitable way (with a fight, flight, or freeze response) to enable us to survive. If the system was activated in childhood due to an adverse experience, we now understand due to the developmental learning in neuroscience, the brain's neural pathways retains the fact that we did survive it, and therefore that response (whatever it was we did) is the best response to use to overcome the current threat (without thinking). Over time, it becomes the automatic response that is triggered without conscious thought, and sometimes when there is no real or active threat, the limbic system is reminded about the trauma, and it worries it might be happening again. The most appropriate response for the individual that worked in the past is what the person accepts as the usual response, and it becomes the 'normal response' for them.

THE NEURAL RESPONSE TO TRAUMA

When an individual is in a familiar environment, and feels safe, the limbic system is relaxed (or not active) generally. The primitive and limbic systems generally do the functions that are needed to survive, for example, heart pumping, lungs breathing, while we continue focusing on everyday activities such as reading, cooking, cleaning, communicating, sleeping, etc. However, if we enter an unfamiliar environment or sense an internal threat, the limbic system activates our ability to unconsciously scan the room for risk. One might experience a sense of restlessness, hypervigilance, or may not be able to be completely relaxed. When this system is activated, depending on the intensity of the threat, one might also notice changes in bodily sensations often associated with chemical (neurotransmitter) changes that have been caused by this sense of threat. If the threat is sensed and one does not feel safe, butterflies in our tummies, feeling sick or a sense of nausea, heart beating faster than normal, sweaty sensations, etc., may not be noticed. The limbic system is preparing the body to respond to the sensed threat through the usual fight-flight-freeze response. This is a normal or natural response to a sense of threat or trauma. The common response to the threat is the usual fight-flight-freeze. However, there are actually two further responses that one might have when experiencing a traumatic event: flop and friend. Exploring all five of these responses can help us make better sense of the reactions.

Fight is when the belief system is, "I am bigger, stronger and can win against the person. I will stand my ground and win". **Flight** is a when the belief kicks in, "I am smaller and will not win. I can get away though, so I'm going to run". **Freeze is** when the belief is, "I can't get away and I can't win. I'll freeze because if I don't respond they may lose interest and go away". It could also be in response to an event that is so sudden or unexpected that the individual has no time to think and may simply freeze. **Flop** is when the initial response may be a freeze, but then the threat is not going away; staying frozen is going to hurt, so flopping and playing dead is the response, with the hope it will be over soon, and the threat will go away. **Friend** is where there is a realisation that the individual cannot stop the threat, so the belief kicks in that keeping the person on my side – or being friendly – will keep the situation happy or they may notice less resistance, therefore they won't hurt me as much. The freeze, flop, and friend are the common responses to any kind of abuse (especially if it is chronic) and/or outside the control (internal and external) of the person experiencing trauma.

So, when the brain (i.e., limbic system) senses any threat, and within milliseconds – our response is physical and our belief system (based on past experiences) kicks in. If the assessment is not a threat, the body notices that momentary spike in adrenalin or that fast heartbeat or the skip of a beat and then settles back to being calm. Very often when we sense the threat, either the automatic belief, "it's safe, I can deal with this", or "Oh-Oh, I did not manage this last time" is triggered, and usually the pre-frontal cortex initiates logical response. But if we sense the threat (because of our past experiences or trauma), the emotional brain takes over, and our logical or reasoning brain does not function as it would when we are not faced with a threat because the frontal lobe is not applying the brakes (or inhibit) our emotional response. This process, that we go into in the split second when we need to survive a traumatic experience, is a complex pathway (see Figure 2.1).

Whenever someone experiences, a traumatic event, the perceived threat to their life is extreme, their survival response gets triggered. For example, when someone senses an unwanted sexual touch (in any form), unconsciously they will assess the situation to decide whether they can fight. If they feel their attacker will back down or they are stronger this may resolve the situation, and they will, although impacted, be safe. If they cannot 'fight' they will assess whether they can flee, and get to safety, also sometimes known as 'flight'. If that is not possible, for whatever reasons, the next response is a 'freeze' response. However, there is no order of preference for selection of these responses, as it happens in less than few milliseconds. If they do freeze, then everything basically stops at that point – the sense of time, thinking, and any emotional response. The connection between

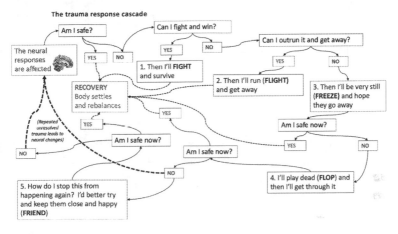

Figure 2.1 The five responses to trauma

the limbic system and cortex is disconnected, and the individual may not be able to think logically or respond. The sense of survival might be so strong that they may not be able to remember the details of the attack. In this example, as there may be some form of sexual contact, some individuals may notice or sense the physiological response of pleasure or sensation, which they may remember and over time may feel guilty, as this was unwanted. The physical form of the body may respond with pleasure, but the cognitive and emotional part disconnect as it's not consensual. Experiencing any trauma where the response is that of a flop might lead to individuals often experiencing or feeling disconnected from their bodies and reporting that they have no memory of what happened. This is often referred to as dissociation (for details see Chapter 4).

After the first traumatic event it can take a long time to feel safe again and the brain will continue to be on high alert, scanning for potential danger after the event. If another traumatic event occurs before we feel safe again or if the individual is in a situation where similar events happen more regularly, the individual's neural pathways learn and will automatically use the 'best' survival response as the default response. If the traumatic event happens during early childhood or developmental periods, the automatic response is what helps them to survive, and the belief system is developed along the lines of, "this is the best way for me to survive". As the individual has not been able to feel safe and calm, the threat system is still on, the individual is unable to downregulate this and has not been able to rest and recover. This leads to the individuals being more aware of and alert to their surroundings, often scanning for threats; this is termed 'hypervigilance'. Being always aroused, not being able to downregulate, is exhausting for them, and in the long-term impacts on their sleep, well-being, and physical health.

In simple words, the threat system is like a torch. When walking at night we may not need it until we are in a street where there is no light or when we are looking for something that we might have lost – that is, scanning. But if I am walking and I constantly feel threatened, I am going to keep my torchlight on – for safety. Now if it's always on, the battery is going to die soon enough. The next day, I would not feel safe without the torch. Over time, I cannot walk out without that extra light – which is the hypervigilance – in our system. If we understand this response, then it helps us find ways to pause or rest or learn we do not need to be hypervigilant all of the time, but only when needed, not 24/7, 365 days a year.

One useful tool to understand this is the concept of 'window of tolerance', adopted by Pat Ogden et al. (2006, see Figure 2.2). This helps us or our clients understand how their alarm system is working and identify whether they experience periods of calm, rest, and relaxation. If we can regulate the alarm system consistently, then when we do not notice a threat, or feel safe, we will stay within the 'window'. The frontal lobe (thinking brain) can continue to engage in decision making, planning, inhibition, emotional regulation, etc., and we will notice the blips, or high and low emotions, but feel generally okay. However, if one is not able to regulate their alarm system or switch off the hypervigilance, then, the alarm system takes over, the capacity to think and rationalise is lost, with the individual being out of the window of tolerance, either on the top (hyper-arousal) or at the bottom (hypo-arousal), feeling low.

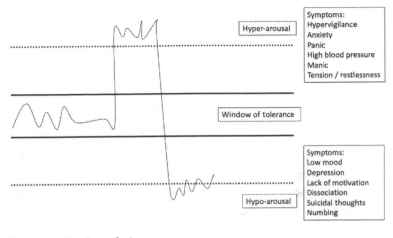

Figure 2.2 Window of tolerance

Source: Adapted from Ogden et al. (2006)

Another helpful concept that can be used to support our understanding of how our limbic system is constantly scanning our environment to assess safety is the polyvagal theory (Porges, 2011). This theory is useful because it brings together the defensive or survival responses of fight-flight-freeze-flop-friend alongside the neurological mechanisms of activating the nervous system. The vagus (cranial) nerve is the main part of the parasympathetic nervous system. Traditionally the nervous system is split into two, the 'sympathetic' nervous system – which is more about responding or being activated (flight/flight) – and the 'parasympathetic' – which is more about regulation and health. Polyvagal theory (Porges, 2011) suggests a third additional function of the nervous system, termed 'social engagement', which allows us to assess whether there is any threat to our safety when we are engaging with others.

Polyvagal theory describes social engagement as a key aspect of our brain's way of assessing danger. It gives us the language to describe how the nervous system is constantly analysing environmental information and that the body can often feel threat through the whole limbic system before we can think (in the cortex) about whether that threat is real.

Sayings in our culture like "trust your gut", "gut instinct", and "I feel it in my waters" go some way to describe how we can trust our bodies to know if we feel safe. The problem we face in trauma is that we often discount these feelings as being "silly", "wrong", or "dramatic". Specifically in relational trauma or abuse we may have been told that what we feel in our body is incorrect – so, for example, if we haven't felt safe with someone because they are shouting at us we are likely to be activated, our defensive response of fight or flight might kick in, we might try and tell them to stop, shout back, or perhaps get out of the room. We might then have been told, "what is wrong with you, you are okay – I'm not going to hurt you!" so we begin to get confused and disconnect our own body reactions. Learning to notice and assess our own internal reactions from this perspective can be very helpful.

There are two separate branches of the polyvagal nerve which runs from our intestinal system (guts) to our brain. These branches are called the 'ventral vagal' and the 'dorsal vagal' system. The ventral vagal supports our social engagement and is aligned with allowing us to assess whether we feel safe enough with the people around us to engage with them, and feel connected or grounded by enabling us to unconsciously read body language, facial expressions, and emotional response from the other. If we begin to feel uneasy, our arousal level increases and we then move towards the possibility of activating our fight-flight response. There is still capacity to act at this point. If we can resolve the threat then we will downregulate and return to a state of safety and connection. The dorsal vagal aspect, however, is more aligned with when we cannot act to resolve the conflict, and we need the more extreme survival responses because we have determined that we really do feel threatened and the limbic system's mechanisms are switched on. It is this part that activates our freeze-flop response as it is closely linked to the parasympathetic nervous system. It is also what can help us recover and heal after experiencing trauma, as the recovery and downregulation is a key aspect of processing the triggering event. Figure 2.3 (adapted from Stephen Porges, 2011) illustrates the whole concept and shows how when we are activated (the bell curve) we move through the different levels of response.

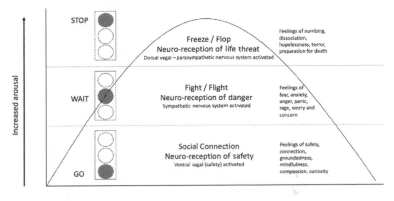

Figure 2.3 Adapted polyvagal theory

Source: Porges (2011)

PHYSICAL, PSYCHOLOGICAL, AND SOCIAL RESPONSES TO TRAUMA

When an individual experiences any trauma, be it physical, sexual, emotional, or a natural disaster, their response to that event varies. Some people may only experience one symptom of the possible psychological responses, while others may have more than one (see Figure 1.2). The onset of the PTSD symptoms may not always be immediate; this can be seen when someone is triggered by a recent experience (e.g., a recent bomb blast), but has been a veteran and served for years in the army and never experienced the symptoms of PTSD before. But while watching the news of a recent terror attack in the comfort of their home, whilst having a cup of tea, out of the blue, the person is triggered and re-experiences all the past trauma. Many people often think that this sudden re-experiencing does not make sense and wonder what's happening. Using a simple analogy, we all have our personal capacity (think of this like a bucket) of holding the trauma that we might experience, and can carry on with our life. When this capacity is full or reaches its limit, any small event or experience can tilt the whole bucket, or most of it, and we experience the reliving of the past.

This bucket of trauma varies across individuals; if an individual has any insecure attachment (see Chapter 3 for more details), present day stressors, environmental factors, neurodiversity, cultural implications (see Chapter 4), or other traumatic experiences, the bucket may have holes or cracks, which further contributes to the bucket's capacity. Often, when PTSD symptoms have been triggered, the individual's hypervigilance tends to switch on. Without support it may be difficult for them to regulate this heightened alertness, which can lead to both mental and physical tiredness. During this phase the individual may experience other symptoms and often remains outside their window of tolerance (see Figure 2.2). In cases where the individuals have sought professional help or mended some of the cracks, they heal and hold the trauma better. Over time with long-term counselling or other family support, the individual can almost empty the water (trauma) from that bucket and re-engage with life.

The psychological effects of trauma include individual negative experiences, such as shame, guilt, and anger, and often the society's expectations that one 'should' be able to get on affects the person's self-esteem and ability to relate to the other, which can lead to thoughts such as, "why me?". If they experience guilt, then they may experience a sense of "I do not deserve to be happy", or "I should not feel any happiness". In clinical language, we might refer to this as 'victim blaming'. For example, one may hear that the person was raped because of her dress or behaviour. The expectation that the victim's behaviour was a reason for the trauma to happen could further affect the recovery journey. When the individual experiences any physical, emotional, or psychological effects of the trauma, they find it difficult to trust the system or people. Often as the inner self or when they were a child, they had to find the mechanisms to survive by themselves and could not rely on the safety from a primary carer.

In addition, an aspect that is often overlooked is the physical impact of trauma. When we experience something that is not okay, but we are not able to – for whatever reason – process this or talk about it, we hold the trauma in our bodies. This might mean that we have pain in our body that is unexplained; for example, many trauma survivors will experience pain in their muscles or joints. This is investigated medically, and people might receive a diagnosis of fibromyalgia or chronic pain, or they might have digestive issues such as irritable bowel syndrome or Crohn's disease (Van Der Kolk, 2014; Levine, 2010). When these clients present for therapy, they are asked in a different way about their relationships, their early experiences, and the traumas they may have had to manage alongside the physical complaints as adults, and we can begin to recognise the possible impact on their bodies. Clients experience a relief of letting go when they realise the tension they hold and both authors (AW and SF) have worked with people whose pain or physical health complaints resolve greatly during their therapy. One client who worked with AW comes to mind here. When she first arrived for therapy, she was 50 years old and morbidly obese, with a long list of physical complaints that included diabetes, fibromyalgia, chronic pain, crumbling back, high blood pressure, lupus, angina, and many more. Over the course of the work, having been given the space and time to explore how these things were affecting her life, she was able to recognise when the health conditions that were related to pain began and how this might have been because of the sexual abuse she experienced. She had held the shame, secrets, and the sense of being 'bad' internally and that had turned into physical pain. She exclaimed, "Well, it had to go somewhere I guess!". She also recognised that she had begun to put on weight around the same time to make herself 'unattractive' to men. By making these connections she was able to identify why she had never been able to lose weight – it would have been too dangerous for her to do this. What if she then became attractive! She was then able to make different sense of her current situation, knowing that she did have choice and control over aspects of her life now. Over time she lost weight and her physical health conditions improved so much that by the end of the therapy with AW she had reduced her medications significantly, managing her diet and health very differently. AW's reflection with the client at the end of the work focused on the change in her physical appearance and health. This had been made possible by the client understanding the trauma reactions that had been stored in her body and it was by knowing this that she gave herself the permission to make different choices as an adult.

There is now a growing body of work (in both research and clinical practice) that views trauma held in the body as key to recovery. There are therapeutic training and theories that support working with the body to understand the full impact of our traumas (e.g., sensorimotor psychotherapy, founded by Pat Ogden), and practitioners of many complementary or alternative therapies such as yoga, Pilates, massage therapy, reflexology, etc., now recognise the impact on the body when working with their clients. They utilise similar theory and practice to think about how to release trapped trauma and regulate emotions when working with their clients. How the person heals or mends their experience(s) is informed by their individual, cultural, and environmental factors. Some may prefer to just reinforce the cracks on their bucket, while others may want to create a bigger vessel which holds the broken parts as well as the new. Or someone else might use the experience as a metaphor for life and reinforce their experience and strengthen their capacity by making it more valuable, like the Japanese practice called kintsugi, which uses precious metals to repair broken pottery, symbolising viewing life's broken experience as an opportunity to reinforce and develop your own character (see Chapter 6 for more details on recovery).

3

ATTACHMENT AND TRAUMA

Childhood experiences influence how we respond when faced with any traumatic or adverse event(s). Attachment to the significant carer is the key to how the child develops and copes throughout life. Bowlby's early work (1969) discusses the four basic attachment patterns, defined as secure, avoidant, ambivalent, and disorganised. The key work on attachment was presented by Bowlby in the trilogy *Attachment and Loss* (1973, 1980, 1982), while Ainsworth et al. (1978, 1982, 1989) brought the research perspective. The model of attachment (in adults) is often thought to be described along the lines of attachment to oneself and others. It was initially thought that one cannot change these attachment styles, but evidence suggests that when individuals are aware of their attachment patterns, with support, they can reorganise their attachment style(s). The attachment developed during childhood often affects how the child responds to any situation both during the childhood period and adulthood. However, if a child experiences any accident or natural disasters (e.g., tsunami, terrorism, etc.), it would be classed as an adverse childhood experience, and how the child responds to that is based on several factors, including the early attachment patterns, the currently safety or security of the child, and the child's resilience based on their early experiences. This chapter provides an overview of how attachment relates to trauma and reflects on how psychotherapy can help shift attachment patterns in adult life.

DOI: 10.4324/9781032637242-4

WHAT IS THE ROLE OF EARLY CHILDHOOD EXPERIENCES IN TRAUMA?

The early attachment style is known to affect the individual's perspective of self and others and how they respond in social situations. When a child experiences trauma during early periods in life, it will change some of the neural responses in the brain. When the infant is born, the attachment is not automatic; consistent and reliable attunement from a caregiver is needed for the infant to feel safe (Solomon, 2011) and for the attachment to begin to develop. Fisher (2021) reminds us that human babies are born with limited capacity; the external support allows them to regulate their nervous systems and recover from any distress. This experience in turn allows the baby to recognise and tolerate positive feelings towards it. Specifically, the capacity for affect tolerance is thought to be developed in the first two years of our life (Fisher, 2017; Schore, 2003). Steele et al. (2016) suggest (p. 61) that by providing 'good enough' attachment a parent or caregiver teaches the baby that they are safe to be soothed by others, and that it is safe to sooth our own self, when loved ones are not present. This links to Erikson's (1994) developmental stages, where when a crisis is resolved at each developmental stage, the child is better able to cope and has a secure relationship. Infants and children are incredibly able to sense emotions and perceive the environment they are in. We know that children develop their innate attachment behaviour from the environment and the social engagements with their caregivers. From birth, a form of self-regulation pattern often develops; this in turn feeds into the arousal within that child (Beebe, 2010). The child with a secure attachment to the primary caregiver(s), when faced with uncertainty or arousal, learns to be curious and rely on their own self. If the child in distress is soothed, they learn from the experience, building resilience.

There is a fundamental difference in a child's response to a secure or anxious parent. Secure attachment derives from the child living with people that they 'know'. The people around them and their nervous systems are regulated in their environment; they are supported and soothed when needed. By comparison, insecure attachment arises when the child is living with people who are 'strangers' to them. Hughes states, "babies who live with strangers do not live well or grow well" (Hughes, 2018, p. 3). The key driver in the development of this attachment is the survival instinct. This is often discussed in the context of trauma as the flight or fight responses (Cannon, 1929) which is explained physiologically in the light of polyvagal theory within trauma response (Porges, 2011). Positive experiences such as being fed, stroked, rocked, held, positive eye contact, bodies touched, and played with (e.g., tickling, raspberry blowing on tummies) all create our sense of safety and attachment to others. In contrast the negative things we can experience such as anger from the caregiver, lack of eye contact, tension in the body, lack of warmth in the face, loudness, and tone of voice, etc., can begin to develop fear in the young child and a sense of insecurity. A negative stimulus, such as a loud noise, a shout or sudden movement will startle and/or scare a baby. Their nervous system responds to this stimulus and the sense of being threatened is experienced. This feeling is tolerated, if the child has a sense of safety and security with their caregiver; if not, this is experienced as 'traumatic', with the development of a sense that, "they [the child] do not feel okay, they are not safe". The internal model of attachment (Fisher, 2021) goes on to suggest that the infant's sense of self is determined by and in relation to the carer's willingness and ability to read and respond to the baby's needs. An infant instantly searches for the gaze of the other. Babies will move their heads to search for the eyes of the caregiver, so that they know that they are there, and that they are safe. During this eye contact, if they do not feel reassured or safe, but instead this contact makes them feel scared, their nervous system is not brought back into regulation and instead becomes dysregulated. The baby will, in these circumstances, do what they can to move away – they will close their eyes or turn their head away or find a behaviour that helps them survive the experience.

Case Examples:

I (SF) often use an analogy of my dog (Franklin) when talking about trauma, given that often the response to trauma is very instinctive or based on the need to survive. Franklin is currently 2.6 years old, and he experienced trauma in the first 6 weeks of life and did not develop a secure attachment with his dog-mother or the breeder. His natural response was to bite; when we got him, he often looked for that safety with our older dog (Toffee) and myself. If he felt threatened and anxious, he would redirect or displace the internal chaos to behaviours like biting the lead or jumping aggressively. Over time as he developed a secure attachment, we noticed he would look at us and expect positive eye contact, and he was able to then, over time, calm down sooner and get on with the walk.

As adults one often uses the attachment pattern(s) learnt as children; if we are fearful of contact with others, it may be hard to make eye contact or engage socially. A client who had been working in weekly therapy for more than 3 years (with AW) once commented, completely out of the blue, "You know, if someone asked me what you looked like I wouldn't be able to tell them. I don't think I've ever looked at you". She had a disorganised attachment style and even though she could say that she trusted the therapist when she was with her in the therapy room, she still could not bring herself to look and risk making eye contact. Fisher (2021) discusses this in relation to developmental trauma. When eye contact is scary because the child (or baby) was not responded to, they feel terrorised in their initial eye contact with their caregivers; this may be traumatic and the beginning of insecure attachments. One way to consider this is that if the child experiences their caregiver as frightening or senses anxiety in the relationship, the child in turn will become chronically afraid of being hurt (Fisher, 2021). They may become sensitive to things that other children are not sensitive to, often being told that they are 'overly sensitive' or 'too emotional'. Any sense of being rejected will trigger big emotional and physical responses of fear, shame, and anger, thus reinforcing the child's negative experiences.

The affect tolerance is thought to be directly tied to the attachment developed in early years, and feeds into the autonomic nervous system

(Ogden et al., 2006; Siegel, 1999; for more details see Chapter 2, Neuroscience of trauma). If a child develops an attachment style which is one of the three insecure types (avoidant, ambivalent, or disorganised), when faced with trauma(s) the reactions will be linked to the predominant or implicit way of relating to others based on the attachment. When a child is left to manage the consequences of any adverse event on their own, the effect of future trauma will be longer lasting, compared to a child who has had support. For example, a client who has an insecure ambivalent attachment to their primary caregiver will not be able to predict the other's response in the face of trauma. The person will then try to work out how best to elicit the care by trying to respond to what others might expect, instead of being connected to their own needs. This often then results in their needs not being met. They reject the care offered, which reinforces their belief that they are not 'good enough' and that 'no-one will help anyway'.

The early bonding experiences are remembered implicitly and known as 'emotional memories' that are felt in the body as the individual develops. When the trauma or the source of danger is the attachment figure, then there is a need for the child to still survive within the dysfunctional bond. The individual then internally mobilises the survival responses to protect themselves. It is here, when the defence mechanisms are activated in the context of trauma, that one often sees elements of repression (Freud, 1957).[1] Repression may be either of the event itself, where the adult develops selective amnesia, or of the emotions associated with it.[2] In either case, this suppression (or repression) of the traumatic environment may lead to a perception by the individual that such an environment is normal. These childhood responses frame the adult patterns of relating, for example, relationships where there is trauma or abuse being perceived as normal and tolerated. Therefore, it is comparatively straightforward to see that if our attachment style is secure the impact of trauma when it happens will be less than if our attachment style is that of one of the insecure types. The early attachment style, therefore, contributes to how well we can regulate our nervous system and lessen the impact of trauma on our lives.

ATTACHMENT AND THE HUMAN BRAIN

From birth, the human brain is continuously developing and changing. In early years, neurons form connections, and synaptic pruning occurs (i.e., a process where unused connections are eliminated (Tau & Peterson, 2010; Huttenlocher, 1984). Neural connections that are used frequently get strengthened during the early years of development. It is not only early childhood experiences that shape the human brain but also neuroplasticity (the ability to change the brain network), which continues to occur into adulthood.

The emotional brain is the primitive brain region that humans share with animals; however, the frontal brain is what has evolved in humans making us unique in our ability to reason and think logically. The limbic system (also known as the Papez circuit, 1937) which forms part of the midbrain, is a complex network for controlling emotions, and includes structures like the hippocampal formation, the amygdala, the septal area, hypothalamus, cingulate gyrus, and parahippocampal gyrus. The hypothalamus is known to regulate the autonomic nervous system via hormone production and release. It is the frontal lobe and areas within the prefrontal cortex that regulate and control our instinctive behaviour. When faced with a threat (one-off or repeated), our nervous system automatically goes into either the fight, flight, freeze, and in some cases into the flop or friend response (see Chapter 2 for more details). Often this response is based on our learnt experiences and environment. For example, when a person sees a large dog and has no prior experience, they may be curious or cautious. However, if they have been bitten in the past, they would go into a flight or freeze response. In cases where they are familiar with managing dogs, they would be more confident of confronting the large dog; they may go into a fight or a positive response.

If this example is explained through the context of trauma, the instinctive response allows the individual to tolerate moments of trauma, after which they may regulate and relax. After the emotional brain responds to that traumatic or adverse event, the prefrontal cortex comes back online and begins the emotional, and sometimes physical, healing process. If our early attachment is secure, the individual is more likely to trust others in times of crisis, whether that be emergency service personnel, friends or family, and even complete strangers. The implicit awareness is that they can be safe, soothed, and cared for. Over time, the nervous system regulates itself. Although there is an impact for a brief time (which varies across individuals), the individual is more likely to recover shortly afterward. However, if the individual's early attachment is insecure, or disorganised in its presentation, then at the time of crisis the nervous system will go into a complete overload, potentially leading to responses like self-isolation, break down, repression, or dissociation to survive. This individual is less likely to trust themselves or that others will be able to help them.

The neural networks in the brain are shaped during the child's early development years, the responses to childhood trauma and attachment. This then influences the behavioural response of the adult, which is normal given the past traumatic experiences and brain networks that have developed as a result. For example, the behaviour response of being hypervigilant was developed in response to surviving a situation where the child felt unsafe. This might continue in adulthood and in turn contribute to mood changes, such as high anxiety or low moods. That individual may not have had the opportunity to learn or even be aware of their behaviour, and that is what they may learn within the therapeutic experience. This is illustrated in a client example below (who presented with neurodiversity).

The client (ST) was a 19-year-old female, who had been in therapy for a number of years, before working with one of the authors (SF). She was sexually abused as a child (by a member of the family) but had a mother who was able to take her away and provide some safety soon after the incident. This client had been in therapy just after the age of 16 years, where her emotions about the event resurfaced. However, during the initial sessions, she found it difficult to integrate the cognitive behaviour sessions into her life, based on her neurodiversity. Having worked with SF for over a year, ST has started to be able to integrate the learning from the sessions into her everyday life. During one of the sessions, ST mentioned how, when walking to work one day, her friend happened to be walking closely behind her and noticed ST walking ahead. Later the friend spoke with ST and said, "why were you looking back, as though someone was following you?" This brought out another level of awareness in ST, as it happened just after we had spoken about her hypervigilant behaviour and the autonomic response of fight or flight in one of the recent sessions. ST brought this into the therapy, and we spent a few weeks paying more attention to it. She reported that, as her hypervigilant behaviour reduced, her anxiety and stress levels were also reduced. She said, "I feel I am not 'on alert' all the time, but I have to learn to trust my instinct when something goes wrong, but also tell myself, I am safe most often and do not need to be hypervigilant on a busy road at 8:30 am".

Developmental trauma such as abuse or neglect from interpersonal or interfamilial relationships is now classified as a specific type of trauma in the United States (Hughes, 2018). Early experiences of trauma will contribute towards the developing attachment style to form psychological messages that influence our life (Berne, 1972). This interaction directly affects the development of neural changes in the human brain, contributing to the way the individual thinks and behaves. Using psychoeducation and the understanding of trauma in the context of brain development and neural responses with the therapeutic context will provide clients the knowledge and support to shift their attachment style(s) (Uhernik, 2016).

CAN YOU CHANGE YOUR RESPONSES OR ATTACHMENT STYLE WHILST IN THERAPY?

In short, yes! The whole premise of undertaking good trauma-informed psychotherapeutic work between client and therapist is to enable this transition or shift. When the therapist offers a consistent and attuned good enough 'other', a learnt secure attachment can be formed. This allows the client to know that they can trust a person, experiment externally with their response in a safe place, while noticing that they are still OK and tolerated. They then learn how to soothe and regulate themselves within this process. Research does support the use of attachment style in clinical practice or psychotherapy (Levy et al., 2011; Levy & Kelly, 2009; Obegi & Berant, 2009). Bowlby (1982) was the first to suggest that the psychotherapist can become an attachment figure or the person with whom the client forms a more trustworthy and reliable relationship in a clinical setting. These relationships within the therapeutic setting or within the client's world, contribute to the shift in the client's pattern(s). This can also happen outside of a therapeutic relationship, for example, if you start a new relationship with someone who has a secure attachment style, they will model consistent care and, if you have an insecure attachment, you can gradually learn how to feel more secure in the relationship.

To illustrate, we use two clinical examples. The first is a client who worked with AW for a period of 4 years. Initially, the client presented with an insecure avoidant attachment style. She found being in relationships was intolerable, was very dismissive of her own needs and those of others. She would often say things like, "well what's the point, they won't be able to help" or "it's just easier to do it myself" when asked if she could ask for support. Over time, AW noticed that the times when her client felt hurt or angry were times when the client's needs might have been missed. By AW noticing and responding to those missed needs and exploring her emotions, the client gradually began to be able to accept support within the therapeutic sessions. She began to express sadness for being on her own and explore her fear of potential relationships. Towards the end of the work, she had been able to make connections and was being supported by a partner in a healthy, attuned, and responsive relationship. She told AW in the last session that her life had been transformed, she no longer felt she deserved only to be on her own, and was able to trust her partner to notice her and attend to her needs. AW reflected that the client had changed her attachment patterns in her adult relationships, first by recognising that she felt secure and safe in the therapeutic relationship and then by bravely allowing herself to be vulnerable with other adults in her external world.

The second example is one of SF's clients who was in brief therapy after a brain injury. During the rehabilitation sessions the focus was to manage the response to and the impact of the injury. This client had no history of domestic abuse or trauma. However, throughout the sessions, she often remarked that she was the "good girl". On exploring this further, we discovered that although she was comfortable with her early years, she often felt that she never could cry or express her fears in the presence of her family (patterns of insecure avoidant attachment). Since she met and married her current husband, the client reported how she had developed a lovely secure attachment with her husband and was able to clearly see how this was different to the relationship with her mother. Within the sessions, she was able to become more aware and pick up on factors that helped her build her boundaries with her mother and experiment with responding differently in that relationship. She brought back into the sessions that her shift in responses only improved their relationship and she was no longer fearful to be herself. Towards the end of therapy, she was able to be herself with her mother, and within the six- to eight-month period had shifted an early attachment pattern and transferred the learning to influence her behaviour from this brain injury context to other areas of life. As the sessions ended, she was able to meet all her goals and get back to the level of work she wanted to return to. SF reflected that even with a one-off traumatic brain injury, the existing attachments can influence the response. SF noticed how by being curious and holding a safe place the client was able not only to shift her attachment with her mother but was able to also learn how to respond to any crisis in a way that helped her cope and manage her life better.

NOTES

1 Repression and suppression are used interchangeably in this book.
2 Emotions may be numbed or dissociated.

4

THE ROLE OF NEURODIVERSITY, CULTURE, AND INDIVIDUAL DIFFERENCES IN TRAUMA

WHAT IS NEURODIVERSITY AND WHAT IS ITS RELATIONSHIP TO TRAUMA?

Experiencing trauma itself is difficult, but simultaneously trying to deal with the personal, cognitive, emotional, and financial repercussions is challenging. As part of a wider society, we can learn to manage these symptoms and experiences whilst coping with the cultural and the societal expectations. When someone may have an experience of neurodiversity or is diagnosed with a neurodiverse condition, they may notice that their brain processes information differently to others. Some of the common conditions of neurodiversity include autism spectrum conditions, developmental disorders, attention deficit hyperactivity disorder (ADHD), specific learning disorders (dyslexia, dyspraxia, dyscalculia, dysgraphia), sensory integration disorder, Tourette's, obsessive compulsive disorder (OCD), auditory processing, etc. If someone has the experience of feeling different in how they understand the world they may, in order not to show that they process information differently, learn to hide this difference. This is also known as 'masking'; the difference is hidden with great effort and energy to fit in or belong. Therefore, if someone then

DOI: 10.4324/9781032637242-5

experiences trauma, they already have a great system set up to utilise their masking skills which will help keep the trauma symptoms away and portray to the world that they are "*Okay*".

As seen in Chapter 2 (Neuroscience of trauma), trauma affects the ability to process emotions; however, when the individual also has a trait (not formally diagnosed) or diagnosis of neurodiversity, it not only affects their ability to process emotion, but also affects their cognitive processes. With the experience of trauma, this is further exacerbated. Within counselling practices, the label or diagnosis is not essential; however, if the therapist is rigid and not flexible in their approach to deal with the differences that these individuals bring, the level of stress in people with neurodiversity increases. A person may not necessarily be neurodiverse, but experiencing trauma along with anxiety or depression is sufficient to mimic symptoms similar to that of neurodiverse conditions such as Attention Deficity Hyperactivity Disorder (ADHD). They may also experience difficulties in sleeping and fatigue, symptoms known to affect day-to-day activities and cognition. Therefore, when working with individuals who may have trauma, using the trauma-informed framework (see Chapter 6) is essential because stabilising by using grounding techniques is necessary before addressing the core trauma aspects.

Often when experiencing trauma, the individual might also be dealing with other comorbid mental health conditions. Using a case example (SF's client) where a 52-year-old transgender woman came into therapy with severe PTSD symptoms from a recent one-off incident of rape. During the assessment and initial sessions, it was clear that the individual was experiencing severe PTSD symptoms from this recent experience. However, during therapy it came to light that she was still dealing with earlier identity issues. Her formal transition from a man to a transwoman, had happened in the last decade. Recently, having lost her job whilst dealing with her symptoms, she had developed agoraphobia and severe anxiety. After a few sessions that focused on the symptoms of the current trauma, we agreed that it would be more beneficial for her to work on some of the identity and anxiety issues first before focusing on the trauma aspect (these were outside the remit of the charity at that point). She therefore planned to access therapy to manage these and then return to work on the complex trauma in the future.

However, while working on the referral through the National Health Service, this client (as many others do) received a diagnosis of borderline personality disorder (BPD) or emotional unstable personality disorder (EUPD). Clients often do not feel that this diagnosis is a true representation of their experience. In this example, when SF looked at the DSM-V criteria for diagnosis (as part of her teaching), this transwoman's symptoms, which SF saw as the manifestation of trauma, had been misinterpreted during her diagnosis. The client had felt she was not listened to, and a diagnosis was made regardless. The diagnosis and labels of personality disorders are controversial, as they carry a huge amount of stigma and judgement and are on a spectrum. Behaviours displayed in people with this diagnosis can also be linked to early relational trauma, so in terms of labelling how can we separate complex trauma from personality disorders such as EUPD or BPD?

The need for diagnosis comes from having to stick to a medical model framework, and the mental health diagnosis is always based on this model via a psychiatrist/mental health team. The DSM-V, which is currently used as a diagnosis model in the medical field, often uses a categorical diagnosis which does not necessarily acknowledge that there may be an overlap or spectrum. Although the ICD-11 has better adopted the spectrum aspect, the DSM-V is more globally accepted for medical categorisation. To prevent misdiagnosis, there are a number of factors which must work together, and the framework needs to integrate the role of neurodiversity and how these symptoms are presented and may vary based on the cause. This is therefore a long-drawn battle, but as therapists, we need not worry about the label itself but focus on identifying, without prejudice or assumption, the aspects to work with the individual on (i.e., the key aspects that are impactful to them) and what that client brings into the session. As a therapist, you want to be aware of the cognitive, emotional, physical, and psychological effects of trauma (in the context of this book or whatever reason the client comes into therapy) and the client's perspective. You need to understand the human brain, think of the presentation from an understanding of the client's culture, any neurodiversity or other sense of self to be able to work in the present. Finally, understanding the link between trauma and the survival mechanisms is the key to coping, and it is this *survival* need that drives any dissociation or split from that traumatic experience, to allow the person to carry on living with their life.

DISSOCIATION AND HOW IT LINKS TO TRAUMA

As we introduced in Chapter 2, dissociation is a very helpful and normal strategy to survive intolerable traumas. The dictionary definition of dissociation is '*the action of disconnecting or separating or the state of being disconnected*'. This definition gives a very good impression of what the human brain is trying to do in the face of trauma or emotional overload within that individual. This attempt 'to disconnect' is a coping mechanism so that the individual does not feel what is happening. Sometimes this is a way for one to *not remember* it (also known as functional amnesia) or we can have a sense (some sort of implicit memory), but not be emotionally attached to the experience.

Dissociation happens at various levels, and most of us probably experience some element of this in our everyday lives! Daydreams or 'going through the motions' of a task without conscious awareness are examples of this. We can drive or walk somewhere and then not remember if we looked before we pulled out into traffic or crossed the road. We can get immersed in an enjoyable task like reading or watching TV and not be aware of what is going on around us. These are all forms of disconnection (or dissociation); the brain goes into the autopilot mode. Dissociation becomes problematic when the symptoms are pervasive and distressing for the individual. For example, you might not remember a conversation with someone, or you might lose hours of your day, or you don't know where you have been or who you have been with, or you find things in your wardrobe and have no memory of buying them. This is terrifying for the person experiencing it, can cause feelings of embarrassment and shame, and therefore this experience is often not shared easily by the individual. Instead, they might try to cover it up by pretending to know or try to work out what has happened, all of which causes additional anxiety. In some cases, the individual may not even be aware that they are dissociating or have disconnected and may only realise it months or years after experiencing the split (Boon et al., 2011).

When one experiences trauma, and if the limbic system in our brain decides that we cannot possibly survive the situation by using one of the common strategies (i.e., fight, flight, or freeze) which may not a safe option, then we use dissociation (a flop response) instead. When this (flop) response is used frequently, as often is the case when the individual may have experienced any childhood abuse (sexual, emotional, or physical), the limbic system learns this is the best response, and as the individual experiences any threat the system will bypass the other survival strategies (fight, flight, or freeze) and go straight into dissociation as a strategy. This also triggers hypervigilance in the individual. Any threat is identified as life-threatening, and the individual may not be able to regulate the system. The flop (or dissociation) is a great coping strategy when the trauma is happening, but the problem occurs when the individual is no longer experiencing the trauma and the response continues. This response continues because, in cases of childhood adverse events, this learnt response was effective and worked, which established a strong neural pathway. As the individual becomes an adult, the danger may no longer exist, yet the individual is not able to regulate the response and dissociation is the automatic or preferred defensive strategy, which may lead to a dissociative disorder. Dissociative disorders are on a spectrum, similar to the autistic or neurodiverse spectrum, and range from normal dissociation to dissociative identity disorder (Steele et al., 2016). The frequency and level of trauma experienced interacting with the available protective factors will determine the severity of the experience of dissociation (see Figure 4.1).

Individuals who experience levels of dissociation above the normal or borderline (BPD) presentation may try to hide the reality of what they are experiencing. Even when an experienced therapist is working with a client, dissociation can be difficult to spot as

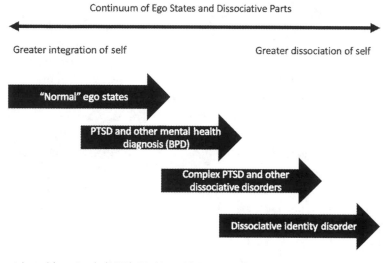

Adapted from Steele (2019), Working with Dissociation Training

Figure 4.1 Working with dissociation training; BPD = borderline personality disorder; PTSD = post-traumatic stress disorder

Source: Adapted from Steele et al. (2016)

the person may not be aware of the split(s) or is highly skilled at masking the presentation. As an example, AW's client who worked for several years with her only felt comfortable enough to disclose the severity of their dissociative symptoms after a significant period. AW noticed this in the sessions and gently brought it to the client's attention. They would go still and quiet for a few moments and then appear to be 'jolted' back into the room, then feel very paranoid that they had done something wrong, yet they still held so much fear about sharing with AW about what was happening for them. After their disclosure, when sharing what had felt so scary to acknowledge, they talked eloquently about the extreme reactions they had had from their primary caregivers when they had lost time, not knowing what they were supposed to say and then being punished by them for 'being difficult and annoying'. Hearing their resistance to their initial experience, it made so much sense why they had tried to hide it for so long. As they experienced a different reaction in therapy, one of compassion and curiosity, they themselves started to notice the dissociative reactions differently, and gradually they started to reduce the frequency of dissociation, initially in the sessions, then in their reality outside the sessions. Towards the end of the work, they would talk about the acceptance and understanding of their dissociative symptoms within the therapeutic relationship which helped them reframe their responses in their here and now. Acknowledging that they had been incredibly resourceful and clever as a small person to survive the horrendous sexual abuse they had endured was transformational. They then realised that they did not need to use that strategy now, as they were safe and could choose their response.

THE ROLE OF CULTURE IN TRAUMA

When talking about stigma across the different cultures it is interesting to note that within some cultures expressing emotion(s) is considered a taboo, while some cultures can accept the emotional expressions and embrace it. Within some cultures, the context of counselling or seeking help may be stigmatised or used as a last resort. The dynamic of culture within counselling will be present irrespective of whether the client and therapist are from similar or different backgrounds. In the context of trauma, the integration of the culture with the individual's unique frame of reference (Raskin & Rogers, 2005) is a catalyst for change. To build a therapeutic alliance, it is essential for the therapist to engage in an active, immediate, and continuous process when working with the culture and ethnic differences.

In practice, when working with multicultural individuals who bring their experience, culture, and belief system, especially in a trauma context — it is difficult to approach this from a top-down perspective. As traditional approaches or frameworks were developed within a Western, educated, industrialised, rich, and democratic (WEIRD) setting, one must break with the norm while maintaining a framework that is flexible and integrates the culture, values, and experiences of that individual. Employing a transtheoretical approach which does not use any particular therapeutic orientation or theory (Palmer, 2001) but integrates with humanistic and existential approaches would support working within the cultural framework. This is an opportunity for the therapist to be curious, learn with the client, and be aware of any judgements that may arise.

For example, it is only in recent years that in some countries there has been an increase in people engaging with psychologists or counsellors to manage their personal dilemmas. Coming from an Indian ethnicity (SF), often I do notice that there are many positives within the culture that can be supportive, but this may vary across the different individuals, their experience, and their perspective of that culture. When in India, or within the Indian community, the boundaries are often much more fluid and, for lack of better words, people would give their opinions irrespective of the impact. When viewed by someone new to this culture, this may appear very intrusive and they may feel that the culture does not respect their personal space, while someone from India in a different place might miss that sense of belonging. Another example may be where people from Italy, south Asia, or Africa thrive in feeling a sense of a community, which may be lost if people move out of their comfort zones to new cultures or places. Also, religious or spiritual beliefs can be positive, negative, or neutral depending on a lot of factors. Often the individual's ability to deal with uncertainty in life may be influenced by the interaction between the environment, cultural or religious beliefs, intergenerational and past experiences. Hence the context of culture within the trauma framework is vital in terms of change and recovery. This sense of culture shapes our identity.

INDIVIDUALS' IDENTITIES (E.G., LGBTQ+ AND TRANSGENDER) AND TRAUMA

Identity is unique for each person; we know that this develops throughout one's lifetime. One's identity not only refers to gender, sexual identity, job, career, etc., but also involves the cultural, ethnicity, experiences, and beliefs that contribute to a person's sense of identity. As humans (Homo sapiens) we evolved about 315,000 years ago from great apes and thrive as a society being comfortable in what may be referred to as 'in-groups'. As we have evolved to creating our own identities, there are pockets of individuals or societies where people with nontraditional identities still are not welcomed. These pockets can establish boundaries based on several factors, including ethnicity, sexual orientation, gender, jobs, and personal experiences. Especially today, with increased global outreach, the cross-cultural elements of migration, race, or ethnic differences have become critical and need to be integrated into the world of counselling. Ford and colleagues (2015) discuss the role of culture, race, sexual orientation, disability, and other factors that contribute to chronic stressors, including social stigma and discrimination in society which contributes to the experience of PTSD or complex trauma.

In the context of trauma, experiencing adverse childhood experience or traumatic events is often not easy to cope with. This coupled with the individual struggling with their sense of identity, means the journey towards recovery and healing has more layers and may take longer. The sense of identity can often be a struggle especially within migrant groups, people with different sexual or gender identities, people who seek refuge coming from other countries or places where there is war or discord. Within a society, we often live with rules that have traditionally existed; any change challenges our existence. This change can come from cultural aspects, ethnic perspectives, or from one's own sexual or gender identity. The first response within any society is to automatically blame the victim (Suarez & Gadalla, 2010), as we expect that the person could have prevented that event or experience. Also, it is easier to blame the victim than to think of the perpetuator, who may or may not be visible. We expect that individuals can influence the action, but seldom realise that PTSD may occur when the individual did not have the capacity to stop and froze or flopped as a response to that event and did not have support to cope. The victim is already dealing with the grief, guilt, and the pain of that trauma and victim blaming – whatever the reason behind it – does not support the person who experiences the trauma and creates more challenges for that person.

OVERVIEW OF THE ROLE OF MIGRATION ON TRAUMA

Over years with the experience of war, conflicts, etc., there is now a growing body of work exploring the effect of migration, including forced migration, asylum-seeking, or any other forms of migration, especially its role when there is PTSD or trauma associated with the shift and adjustment. It is essential when exploring any aspects of trauma to keep in mind the intergenerational legacies of trauma that might have occurred within that community or culture (Wolynn, 2017). Migration in any form can not only affect the individual but importantly also affect children and adolescents who are migrating because of parents and feel a sense of lack of control. When understanding trauma from a migration perspective, the role of attachment both of that individual who is migrating with his or her parents and the style of attachment with their children is also key to keep in mind (Wiese, 2010). Simultaneously also understanding the pull or push for that migration may be important in understanding the individual's experience.

When considering migration as a factor affecting trauma, it is necessary to understand the process of acculturation (Sam & Berry, 2006), which refers to the person having to make psychological adjustments to their environment and culture. When the individual must deal with this, but has had adverse childhood experiences, the beginning of this process does not occur on stable ground (Sourander, 1998). Often when going through the acculturation process complex interactions across multiple dimensions are involved, including the affective, social, and cognitive, and there may be additional stressors, such as lack of support, financial load, etc. (Taylor, 2009; Cohen & Wills, 1985; Wiese, 2010; Wiese & Burhorst, 2007). When migration happens, the individual must strike a balance between this shift in the new environment and also keeping up with the culture back home. When trauma happens, it would not be easy for the individual to deal with shame, guilt, anger, and other negative feelings and the individual might want to suppress or repress it to survive and manage day-to-day life.

WHAT IS THE ROLE OF TRAUMA-INFORMED COUNSELLING IN SUPPORTING DIFFERENCE AND DIVERSITY?

The main ethos of a trauma-informed approach in therapy is to enable the individual to have a safe, nonjudgmental space to process the impact of what has happened to them and the symptoms that they are experiencing as a result, without the need for labelling/ diagnosis or stigma. Effectively phased trauma-informed therapy focuses on the individual and enables curiosity into the impact of their trauma symptoms and the internal belief system that the person has because of their experience. Their self-beliefs will also be based on any cultural influence or neurodiverse traits that they may have.

Using the phased approach (Herman, 1992) as a framework (see Chapter 6 for details) a key milestone is the building of the therapeutic alliance, co-creating a shared understanding that incorporates all the aspects of the client (cultural, experiential, developmental, etc.), which then allows the client to develop the skills to regulate their emotion. This approach supports the journey of recovery from trauma, which is the essence of this framework, while many alternative treatment methods are more goal orientated, formulaic, or outcome focused. Whilst for some clients these alternative approaches may be extremely helpful, they do not accommodate easily for client's who may process information differently (e.g., neurodiverse) – for whatever reason that might be. This means issues of cultural differences or neurodiversity are pushed aside and neglected, potentially causing, at best, relapse once the therapy is concluded and, at worst, reinforcing the negative unconscious views about the differences that individual may have. The beauty of the trauma-informed framework is that each therapeutic relationship will be unique, ensuring unconscious bias is challenged, stigmas talked about, and a curious space created to gently challenge beliefs about the self, while recognising the individual's ability to regulate, supporting the client's journey towards recovery.

5

. . . IS IT TRUE? DEBUNKING THE MYTHS AND TABOOS AROUND TRAUMA

A main driver to write this book was to help redress this balance surrounding the myths and taboos of trauma. Helping friends and family understand the prejudices and judgements that are routinely held about experiencing trauma can ultimately be the final jigsaw puzzle piece for someone who is on their own journey to recovery as being accepted for who they are, not what has happened, which is such a validating experience. Hearing clients say things like, "I told my partner that thing you said about my nervous system always being on and they totally got it, and now we have thought of some ways so that I can let them know when I am feeling triggered, rather than just reacting like 0–100" is fantastic. The client is demonstrating that they are not holding so much stigma about how they respond when they are activated and that they have the confidence to start to share with others what happens for them and state their needs about what is helpful so that they feel safe. Debunking myths and stigma is critical to the progression of trauma recovery.

COMMON MYTHS AND TABOOS AROUND TRAUMA

Myth #1: Individuals who have experienced trauma are being defensive or are perceived by others (and service providers) as being difficult.

DOI: 10.4324/9781032637242-6

Individuals who may have experienced *severe* trauma may often have very high defence strategies that are designed to protect or safeguard their inner self. However, when individuals use these strategies, they can be perceived by others (and service providers) as being difficult, especially if the individual does not feel safe or confident enough to be vulnerable and would rather be perceived as difficult. This often acts as a barrier for them to access care and other services to help their recovery. The individuals are then blamed for their behaviour and scapegoated as a 'bad person'. As discussed, earlier, victim blaming makes it easier to believe that the person who experienced the trauma is bad rather than that terrible things have been done to them. Many people may not have ever received a PTSD diagnosis despite experiencing the symptoms, or even consider that how they live and relate is linked to the trauma they have experienced. They assume that what is said or believed about them being 'difficult', 'a burden', or 'highly sensitive', etc., is correct and this is reinforced through their day-to-day experience. Therefore, the internal shift to not blaming themselves (that happens in phase 1 of trauma-informed work) when clients understand that their unconscious system has been working super-hard to keep them safe (and that it's done an amazing job!) is truly transformational (Gonzalez, 2018). It is frustrating that it has often taken years of someone's life before they are able to fully integrate and understand the impact of what has happened to them, usually due to how they have been treated by society.

Myth #2: It happens, get over it!

Another common issue faced by people recovering from trauma, is when others expect them to 'get over it'. This may also in some cultures be perceived with the assumption or myth that "trauma only affects the weak". This myth is very prevalent in the world of professionals who may work in high demand careers or face traumatic experiences every day, like medical professionals, first responders, teachers, police, army, air force, navy personnel, or veterans where they are *expected* to be strong and showing their vulnerability is considered weak. This is not only the perception of others but also that of the individuals, as they may discount the impact of their experience and brush it off and assume that they can get over it. The fact is that expressing emotions need not be considered as a weakness and being vulnerable is okay. This is something that needs to be addressed at all levels in the society. When one experiences trauma or a series of events that may be traumatic, it is only natural that individuals may feel the pain or the impact; how one deals with it may vary, but it is important that it is acknowledged. Very often individuals may not have had the experience of being held or hearing that it's okay to be not okay. As a society, be it in families, schools, universities, or workplaces, we often want to perform – the feeling of being vulnerable is thought to be weak and not a strength.

Myth #3: Everyone who experiences trauma will definitely have PTSD.

Interestingly, from both research and the personal anecdotal evidence of trauma sufferers, we know that people who may experience trauma, for example, someone who has been in war areas and seen death every day, may not necessarily always immediately experience PTSD. PTSD may occur at any point, however, and it could be because of a completely different trigger. In general, the possibility of a one-off experience of trauma leading to a diagnosis of PTSD or developing PTSD is much lower, and is dependent on several factors, including attachment, early childhood experience, the person's own resilience or motivation, and the current situation they may be in. So, for example, if there were two individuals who experienced a trauma (may be assault or a natural disaster) if they had the same background and childhood experience, but one is currently experiencing a really stressful life experience or struggling with something at a personal level, the chance that this individual will develop PTSD is higher than for the other individual who may be in a more secure and safe place. Therefore, it's not only the previous experience and genetics but also the current life circumstances, social support, and environment that contributes to the risk of developing symptoms of PTSD. Also, the individual's ability to cope using adaptive strategies compared to maladaptive ones will be a positive strength for that individual to be able to cope with the experience of a traumatic event.

If a child experiences a traumatic event or physical, emotional, or sexual abuse either at a very early stage of development (up to 2 or 3 years of age), they may not necessarily have an explicit memory (also often referred to as episodic memory) of that event. In other cases, if the child had experienced a similar event after 3 years of age, they might have suppressed (or unconsciously repressed) that experience to survive or cope with that situation. However, the emotional experience of this, including feelings of guilt, shame, or other negative experience, may still be implicit in the individual's awareness. In cases of people who may have dissociation, they may recognise the period in which the initial split may have happened but may not have details of that experience. Often the myth is that is they don't remember it; they do not need to deal with it. However, if in the future they either experience a similar event or engage in a therapeutic relationship or even engage in a more secure personal relationship, very often this memory, both the felt sense of emotion and the flashback of that experience, might come back into the individual's awareness, and they would have to work to be able to reconnect with their sense of self.

Myth #4: Another myth often heard is that if the individual appears to be okay, that is, well dressed, engaging, is managing in a job and seems to be dealing with life, then the trauma or the adverse event does not impact or may not have impacted them.

The fact is that people who may experience trauma may also have higher ability to cope – which may not necessarily be an adaptive strategy. So, in this case, the individual may either be masking, so they are aware of the impact, but cannot deal with it and hence are carrying on with their day-to-day life. In some cases, the individual may avoid engaging with intense emotions and only try to keep up with the bare experience of emotion. Or in some cases the effect of the trauma could be so severe that the individual disconnects or dissociates from the feelings or emotions of that event as they are not yet ready to deal with it. In such conditions, if the individual does engage in therapy, this experience may emerge. Otherwise, they may carry on with their life, until they are confronted with other adverse events, life stressors, or any other triggers, when this might come out with a disproportionate outburst. So, they may experience symptoms of PTSD years after the primary trauma triggering event.

Myth #5: Another common myth or misconception is often that the experience of trauma is bad!

When someone experiences any trauma, as a friend or family member our immediate need is to empathise or sympathise with them. This might also come from our beliefs that we should not be beaten, abused, shot at, or tortured. However, individuals do not choose to experience trauma; it is a result of an event that occurs and is beyond that individual's control. But in some societies or cultures, the individual is often criticised as it is expected that they invite trouble. It is often the victim who is blamed for the traumatic experience rather than the event or the perpetrator being held responsible. This further develops the belief that it is the survivor that is 'bad' and is responsible for this traumatic experience. If the culture is to keep things close to home and not share negative experiences, then this event is often not even acknowledged and the victim often is forced to 'forget' the experience or is discounted. So, for example, being an Indian myself (SF), growing up, the expectation outside my immediate family was that I should be 'girl-like' and should not be outspoken or direct and be submissive. However, having grown up with my grandfather, I was often allowed to be myself and express my thoughts without any restraint. So, when I initially was married into an Indian family, and whenever I expressed my views, my ex would feel insecure, and the common response was that he felt I was too outspoken and confident. This meant that when he was insecure, he might be verbally abusive. Culturally I felt like I deserved to be verbally abused because I was not conforming. Often when trying to make sense of the situation, I would feel I was not heard, and to be able to get out of this situation required me to work on my strength and self-belief. Similarly, if a girl is raped, in many cultures the victim is blamed for that event because of the dress, the behaviour she might have displayed, or that she deserved it in some way. Hence not only is the experience of trauma associated with the term 'bad', but also the victim is not heard or allowed to express the emotion, feeling, or the response. Often the victim is expected not to address her negative feelings but to carry on with life. The fact that any traumatic event is beyond the victim's control is not recognised in society and may cause victim blaming. With support and over time, the individual may be able to cope, learn from, and integrate this experience into their life. It is during this recovery that they may be able to connect with their own strength to recover and heal from their traumatic experience.

Myth #6: It's in your head, you will be fine. Or, I have done it, so can you.

Very often the response to trauma is thought to be a choice, and one seldom realises that it is a bio-psycho-socio-neuro response to the event. If someone is experiencing any kind of PTSD symptoms or has experienced trauma and is responding to it, a conscious switch or reset cannot address it. Very often the victim holds the experience in their perspective and believes that the negative experience is only 'in their head'. This often leads to feelings of doubt, a sense of not trusting their experience, shame and a feeling of not being listened to or heard. In such cases social exposures like the #metoo movement make it easier for them to come out, rather than at the time they experienced it. Their individual experience or feelings are normally discounted not only by their immediate families, but also service providers in some cases.

Because one person can overcome an experience, be it a terror attack, a natural disaster, or a personal traumatic experience, does not mean that everyone can just get over it. However, the norm in some families or culture is for the person to stop experiencing the negative feelings and be expected to move on. The sense of not being listened to or trusted can often lead to breaking down, having melt downs or other physical experiences, including pain, chronic fatigue syndrome, fibromyalgia, irritable bowel syndrome, etc. There are various personal, cultural, childhood attachment patterns and past experiences that determine our response to an event. It is important to acknowledge the individual and allow them to express their experience, ideally without judgement, and giving them a sense of support or acknowledging that it's okay to be not okay. One might need professional support; the client will need time to heal and understand their response to overcome the experience.

IS FACE-TO-FACE BETTER THAN ONLINE COUNSELLING FOR TRAUMA?

The COVID-19 pandemic changed the world in many ways, and it did leave its mark in the world of counselling. Traditionally pre-pandemic, most counselling sessions or psychological assessments were expected to be in person and online services would not have been offered. Most counsellors resisted the online or phone-based intervention, but with the need to offer continued support through the pandemic, there was suddenly a need for a lot more training for online sessions, especially using video-based platforms (i.e., Zoom, Microsoft Teams, etc.). This provision has fundamentally changed the way that therapy can be offered. This shift has also triggered a number of ethical considerations, with evidence supporting the efficacy of online therapy (Stoll et al., 2020). With both authors (AW and SF) having to opt for online sessions with clients having complex trauma, we have seen that online sessions do work, but a hybrid approach of sometimes being in the same room does have benefits, especially when working with complex trauma and dissociation. Some clients may prefer face-to-face sessions, but with financial and other concerns, for example, travelling, some clients prefer online sessions (Smith & Gillon, 2021). Therefore, there is no right or wrong approach; online and in-person sessions have their benefits but also limitations and what may work better depends on several factors, including the therapeutic alliance.

EXPLORING THE STIGMA AROUND THE EXPERIENCE OF TRAUMATIC EVENT(S)

Unfortunately, the experience people often have when they share what has happened to them is negative. This could be due to a few reasons and is usually driven from a place of uncertainty, judgement, fear, or terror. However, when this happens the negative beliefs already held by the individual about the experience of the traumatic event are reinforced, impacting further their sense of identity, self-esteem, and feelings of worthlessness. This negative response can be due to several reasons, some of which we have already explored in earlier chapters but are usually linked to the concept of stigma or stigmatisation. Stigmatisation can also be linked closely with the myths and taboos that exist about trauma (Suarez & Gadalla, 2010). The concept arises because as our human brain wants to make sense of something we will look to find meaning in an event. If it is too difficult to comprehend that 'someone' would intentionally do 'something' to harm another person it can seem more believable, or perhaps is more palatable, to believe that the person that has been affected could have in some way been responsible for, contributed to, or invited the situation.

The concept of victim blaming (Suarez & Gadalla, 2010) can therefore be thought as the root of stigmatisation. Victim blaming transcends cultures and societies and can often manifest alongside other cultural norms or anxieties around the event, thus not allowing us to pick apart victim blaming as a separate aspect. For example, believing that the girl who was drinking on a night out wearing a short dress was in some way 'asking' to be sexually assaulted or that the transgender woman wearing makeup and a dress is doing so to attract attention and therefore of course will also be abused for their choice. Cultural norms also contribute to the concept of stigma, as when we represent something that is outside our normal frame of reference it can feel scary, and we can feel judged for it (Alexander et al., 2004). It is well recognised that the way to tackle any type of stigma is to educate people about the thing being stigmatised, in this case trauma.

By debunking the myths around trauma we can reduce the impact of stigma and increase the support for those that have been traumatised.

STRATEGIES TO MANAGE TRAUMA SYMPTOMS

Individual responses to experiencing a traumatic event may vary based on each person's early childhood experience or attachment styles and many other factors (see Chapters 2 and 3 for details). However, referring to the trauma cloud (Figure 2.1), some of the common symptoms people might experience include irritability, chronic pain, loss of interest, panic attacks, nightmares, loss of a sense of self, insomnia, decreased concentration, mood changes (anxiety or depression), difficulties in interpersonal relationships, and a sense of disconnect or numbing. Not everyone will necessarily experience all the symptoms together, or at the same time, but it is likely that they will be present in some form or another. The presentation will vary based on the individual differences we have already outlined, such as attachment patterns and strength of support.

There are several useful strategies that can help manage these symptoms.[1] Learning what type of strategy works for everyone is key here as our bodies are all different, and what works to calm and regulate one person may not have the same impact on another. The principles of trauma-informed work can be held in mind here when we approach each other with compassion and curiosity to establish what strategies help and support us. The purpose of using strategies (also referred to as grounding, orientation, or stabilising techniques) is to take control of regulating your nervous system, enabling you to stay socially connected (Porges, 2017), like we described in Chapter 2 using the polyvagal theory, or your window of tolerance, if you preferred that theory. Using techniques that support your prefrontal cortex (human, thinking brain) to stay online and functioning allows messages to be given to the limbic system (the amygdala) that you are safe now, you do not need to respond from fight, flight, freeze, or flop, and that you can create space in your body and mind to think and choose your reactions.

Most importantly our limbic system reacts to triggers, and when we are able to control our triggers, we will implicitly know that we are safe. Using our breath and mindful awareness of being in the present supports the activation of the parasympathetic nervous system to relax and recover, automatically calming or downregulating our nervous system. Some broad examples are illustrated in Table 1 (see Appendix 1.1) that can be used as a stabilising or grounding technique that could help calm your nervous system, signalling to your limbic system that you are safe.

However, please note, these strategies are only some of the options available to help you manage your symptoms and, if you are experiencing any symptoms more regularly or have experienced a recent traumatic event, it is important for you to seek professional guidance and input. Please also be aware that it is important that you feel safe when practicing these exercises and have a place which is comfortable for you to use. Try a number of them out at different times. They will not work automatically – particularly if the first time you try them you are feeling very stressed or dysregulated! Practice them and get to know which ones you like or dislike and try out others that might support your emotional system better. In addition, if you are using any substances (e.g., alcohol, cannabis, or other drugs) regularly, do not practice these when you are under the influence. The reason for this is that any substance impacts your nervous system's ability to regulate, and when you engage in any grounding techniques, it is difficult for your brain to understand if a shift in your emotions is because of your practice or the substance. The use of substances is also known to numb your emotional experience and to recover from any trauma, embracing the emotion, safely and with support, is one of the first aspects for healing.

MENTAL HEALTH AND WELL-BEING LINKED TO TRAUMA

'Trauma' is often seen as a separate disorder or condition, and it is not linked or considered when people present to their GP or mental health team with difficult and distressing symptoms. This is changing but we still notice that many clients we have worked with had received a mental health diagnosis that was not given in the context of trauma, or the diagnosis may have been different. Historically most individuals who have experienced any form of trauma and were displaying symptoms of PTSD or CPTSD, along with other mental health conditions, are likely to have had a diagnosis of anxiety, depression, personality disorders, bipolar disorder, psychosis, and many others. In addition to a defined and diagnosed mental health condition some people may also have been experiencing suicidal thoughts or ideations and they may have, on occasion, even tried to take their life. The experience of not feeling 100%, and then being given a diagnosis of a condition that carries stigma with perceived judgement can make the individual feel ashamed of themselves. Especially if they are expected to live up to an expectation or have had to put on a brave face, they may feel it's not okay to be not okay. However, with this book we are hoping to say, it's okay to be not okay.

If you are a family member or close friend of a person who is experiencing trauma, the most important support is to accept them for who they are and what they have experienced. It is the ability to be nonjudgemental and supportive as the person is trying to cope not just with their everyday struggles, but also their financial/work/family life balance that makes the difference. The ability for them to realise that they can get support without questions being asked or judgement will give them the healing space to recover. Also, for you as a reader, understanding the brain processes, the information about trauma recovery, often known as psychoeducation, will help you regulate your own responses when supporting your close loved ones. There are several resources and workbooks that are available to understand the role of trauma and its responses, just ensure you buy it from a reliable source. Knowing and understanding the polyvagal system or the fight-flight-freeze-flop responses when responding to threat, will help you understand how one responds to a threat and how that response continues, recognising that it's not easy for the individual to change overnight. Time, unconditional acceptance, and support are the best help you can provide.

As medical or allied health professions, we often go down the well-known or evidence-based path. However, if we pause for a second and reflect before responding to the client's trauma, we would be able to see that everyone's experience is unique even if they may share other characteristics. Therefore, when working with trauma, you can have a framework, but each client and each session will be unique, and you have to be ready to work with what comes up for each client at that moment in time.

NOTE

1 If you are interested in more resources or training in trauma-focused approaches do visit www.thetipsuk.org.

6

METAMORPHOSIS

Change because of
trauma-informed therapy

UNDERSTANDING THE ROLE OF VICARIOUS TRAUMA

The experience of trauma can bring out symptoms which often in a therapeutic setting can cause vicarious trauma and distress in the therapist, family members, and anyone supporting the person who experienced the trauma. Often, we also notice vicarious trauma in emergency workers or first responders. They may not necessarily be part of the accident or the traumatic event but responding to it and seeing the distress over time can cause them to experience PTSD or trauma symptoms. Therefore, it is important for people in those circumstances to pause and think about self-care and if need be, seek professional help. Very often we discount the effects of vicarious trauma and forget the whole framework of psychodynamic process, specifically the Jungian aspect of collective unconscious and societal architynes. It is therefore important for one to be more tuned in not only to the symptoms that they experience, but also be aware of any physical and emotional changes in themselves. If we recognise that vicarious trauma (or secondary trauma) is a likely consequence of working (or being friends, or in a relationship) with an individual that has experienced trauma then we can also think about steps that

DOI: 10.4324/9781032637242-7

we can take to support ourselves so that we can tolerate the distress of someone else whilst supporting them to be able to manage their process and understand the impact on their day-to-day lives. To do this it is important to ensure that in a professional context you have access to good trauma-informed clinical supervision which can be provided for you from within your organisation or you can choose to seek it out individually or privately.

Clinical supervision is a space, like therapy, where you can, alongside another qualified person, be curious about the impact of the work on you, and reflect as to why you might be working with someone in the way that you are. Supervision is a valuable space in which to check out the unconscious processes that can be in play when working with trauma. As in therapy training, there are various models of clinical supervision that support developing a curious and functional space. It is important to consider when working with a supervisor to ensure that they are working in a way that will support the complexity of the work you are doing with trauma. We have already talked in the early chapters in this book about how when someone is activated, or when their neural pathways are so engrained that they cannot take on the accountability for their own actions, it can feel really difficult for the therapist to stay present and grounded rather than be frustrated by the lack of progress, risking an enactment of the client's trauma. Taking this into supervision and discussing the impact on you, how the process makes you feel, and thinking through the strategies and interventions you could use with your client to facilitate the development of the therapeutic alliance can be helpful. Offering a different experience of compassion and nonjudgement allows the client's own autonomy to develop and strengthen their resilience implicitly (Lee & James, 2012). This process also mitigates the risk of experiencing vicarious or secondary trauma. Tracking your own bodily symptoms, noticing if you start to dream about your clients, or feel that you are experiencing PTSD symptoms when you have not experienced a trauma are critical things to take to supervision and unpack. It allows you to hold someone else's trauma, but to the side of you, not in you (Poole & Greave, 2012). You can witness, but not take on, the true sense of empathy.

This philosophy is also important if you are living with or are the friend of someone who has experienced trauma. It can feel hard to be alongside their dysregulation. We hope that by the understanding you have gained from this book you will be more able to notice your experience and hold unhelpful behaviours lightly whilst staying alongside someone. Therefore, encouraging them to use grounding and stabilisation techniques to help them know that they are safe now, that bad things have happened but that they are not happening now in the present. Having your own support network, either in the form of your own counselling or utilising online forums, friendship groups, and/or medical professional carers groups can give you the resources you need to maintain your resilience. Know that it is okay to take time out, to set your own boundaries, and to model good self-care which will support the person you know, they will admire and respect your boundaries, even if they find it difficult to start off with.

INTEGRATING THE PRINCIPLES OF TRAUMA-INFORMED THERAPY

When we consider aspects contributing to how an individual's body and mind respond, both at the time of trauma and in the days, weeks, and years after, it is not surprising that it can feel like there is little possibility to recover from the experience(s). This is a frustrating situation for those who have experienced trauma and is thankfully incorrect. Both authors, and many therapists that we work with, have seen clients shift and move into psychological and physical places that allow them to live their lives to the fullest and achieve their own goals. We outline the key approaches to therapy in this section, based on humanistic principles, and demonstrate how they are integrated into a therapeutic framework which directly affects the efficacy of the therapeutic alliance. The principles for practice explained here are based on the approach first presented in the seminal text, *Trauma and Recovery* (Herman, 1992), and later developed by other significant trauma therapists, such as Pat Ogden, Bessel Van Der Kolk, Peter Levine, Stephen Porges, Onno Van der Hart, Kathy Steele, and Suzette Boon (e.g. Levine, 1997; Boon et al., 2011). The practicalities are brought together by the authors' own training, clinical practice, and the invaluable network established, The Dorset Trauma Group,[1] where we have shared experiences of merging evidence-based practices with the theoretical principles to inform efficacy in clinical practice.

It is our belief that the underpinning principle for successful trauma therapy is the therapeutic alliance. The alliance is the relationship between therapist and client, it is the felt sense of safety, security, trust, and mutual respect that is co-created and developed over time to allow an intimate space to exist. This then allows both the client and the therapist to safely explore the traumatic experiences/narratives/maladaptive beliefs (*e.g.*, '*I'm a bad person*', '*I deserved it*', '*I should have told them No*') that have, until now, been banished from the conscious thought but has been present in and impacts the client's everyday responses, their self-esteem, and their relationships.

During AW's qualifying MSc dissertation, she tried to describe how she approached developing a therapeutic relationship, which was the key aspect. The feedback given was "*This seems too simplistic, you seem to discount the complexity of the theoretical approach*". It took her a while to understand what the marker meant, as the alliance is not simple, it is incredibly complex and multifaceted; however, what AW has come to understand is that the relationship (and attachment) between two people is not easy to convey in words, it is the absolute felt sense of feeling okay (the I'm okay, You're Okay position from the Okay Corral in Chapter 1) with another trusted person, but that in therapy this importance is easily discounted. Psychological theories explain presentations and symptoms, yet one wonders why sometimes the 'therapy' doesn't work. We can blame clients for 'not being ready' or 'not wanting to change' because it is very difficult to consider the therapist's part in creating a safe therapeutic space. Often it is difficult for a therapist to sit with the experience and reflect on it from a sense of therapeutic alliance. AW still stands by her words in that dissertation (Woodward, 2017) that the alliance is a key, but also recognises that it is both, the therapist and the client approaching the space to create it that makes the difference in good trauma-informed work; it is about creating a secure-enough attachment to allow the process of repair and healing to begin (See Chapter 3).

THE TRAUMA-INFORMED FRAMEWORK

Judith Herman's book (1992) summarised over two decades of her research and clinical practice working (mainly) with women who were survivors of domestic and sexual violence. Her work comes from a women's liberation standpoint and recognises the need to develop a secure-enough attachment with the therapist first before any meaningful processing and change can occur. This supports the importance of the 'relational' experience in a therapeutic alliance, especially when dealing with clients who bring their traumatic experience into therapy. She, and her colleagues at Boston University, devised a framework that can be utilised with any modality of theoretical thinking to treat the symptoms of trauma. This means it does not necessarily matter what the therapist's core theoretical framework is (e.g., transactional analysis, psychodynamic, Gestalt, integrative, person-centred, etc.) as the therapist works within their training or philosophy bringing in their confidence and competence within a progressive safety space to ensure the work is paced. The client is present in the here and now, and they are not re-traumatised by thinking about what has happened to them.

The three phases of the trauma-informed approached are grounding and stabilisation, remembrance and mourning, and reconnection. Clients can cycle between these three phases, so for example, a client may be able to take one experience and engage with grounding and stabilisation, remembrance and mourning, and reconnection, and start this again for some other experience. Others may engage with one phase and work through the three phases over a few years.

The principle is to initially collaborate (phase 1) to understand the impact of the trauma experienced and foster the sense of safety in a therapeutic relationship. This sense of safety along with psychoeducation (which is the sharing of knowledge of the human brain, the way the body responds to any threat, and acknowledging the expected and appropriate symptoms often experienced in the aftermath of trauma) and techniques that would help the individual to downregulate the response, help them feel more grounded and that will support the client to understand the emotional response and triggers. This will often then shift their automatic response to foster new neural pathways and responses. This allows the client to take control and ownership of their symptoms.

AW and SF are always taken aback by the significance of this element of trauma-informed work. Explaining to clients what their body is designed to do to keep them safe, and that their response when faced with a terrifying situation was appropriate, there is a physical impact that is noticeable. In the room, you can see their shoulders begin to lower, releasing tension, their facial expressions relax, and there is a sense of calmness for a moment as people recognise that 'they did good', they survived. More than one of AW's clients has commented at this point in therapy, "so all this is about what happened to me, not actually me?!" SF's client has responded with, "Ah, so this is a normal response, to what I experienced!?" Once this understanding is established, the client can experience a sensation of relaxation and regulation whilst still being able to recognise and respond to real and present danger.

PHASE 1: GROUNDING AND STABILISATION

The 'grounding and stabilisation' in trauma-informed therapy is purely about encouraging the experience of emotional regulation in the therapeutic space and slowly expanding that skill into everyday life. It is about developing the skill to be curious about the triggers, noticing them, rather than pushing them away or being critical of oneself. The normal response to their experience would have been, "Idiot, you did it again, you are so awful!" (not only being critical about themselves, but also bringing in negative emotions). Through this phase the therapist encourages the clients to ask, "Hmm that is interesting, that happened, I wonder why I responded in that way?". This positive shift in response will support the body and the limbic system to know that they are safe and able to engage the thinking or frontal part of their brain. Knowing that they are safe allows them to remember that they did a good job in the past, and when appropriate, relax and make a different choice now. The rate at which one feels in control differs from one individual to another. This phase aims to support the feeling of safety, building the therapeutic alliance, staying socially connected and grounded.

Often it is in this phase that both the client and the therapist can feel frustrated. It is usual for a client in their first session to think that they need to 'narrate their story' to help process it, with the expectation they will magically feel better. However, knowing what we know about the brain, the response to a traumatic event is often not logical, linear, nor does it have a temporal element. If the client remembers the memory) or narrates (i.e., the telling without the emotion) the event(s), without the sense of safety in the moment, the limbic system will be triggered. The client re-experiences the event in the here and now, feeling the original threat, so although the client does benefit from being listened to, the automatic reactions do not necessarily shift, and the client stays in the heightened arousal state when leaving. It is essential not to shut the client down if they begin to narrate their experience, as this will result in their original feeling of being suppressed, silenced, and helpless. However, explaining the neural mechanism and the underlying process will enable the client to notice their body sensations and/responses. Learning to slow down, allowing themselves to be curious, gives them permission to notice and express themselves.

As an example, AW's client initially refused to utilise grounding and stabilisation exercises, as the client felt that "focusing on breathing makes it worse" and that they just wanted to tell AW how awful things had been. This meant that in each session the client's limbic system was re-activated, the client dissociated, and left the session feeling worse than when they had arrived. AW was working hard to ground retrospectively, ensuring that they were leaving safely – which was exhausting and frustrating for both the client and the therapist! The client was angry with the therapist and when encouraged to notice their body response, the client appeared to dismiss any interventions to bring that awareness. This continued for about 10 weeks, and AW was considering ending the work based on the principle of psychotherapy 'do no harm', as the client appeared to be getting worse. AW could not see how the sessions would continue whilst the client did not want to (or choose to) regulate. One week the client seemed different; they were quieter and less confrontational in the room. When AW asked what was happening for them in that moment, they responded with, "I noticed as I was walking up the path that I felt more anxious than I did in the car, I have never noticed that ever before. I didn't realise that I feel even more anxious when I am here than at home. I don't know why that happened, but now I feel worried, what if this isn't going to help?" Weeks of the therapist noticing the changes in the client's body, and the therapists' responses of self-regulation in the room, had been unconsciously observed and taken in by the client. They had, in that moment, shown AW that they were noticing their emotional affect, and this was a huge milestone in enabling them to explore what helped the client to feel less anxious when engaging within the therapy. They recognised that it's not about the narration, but about being present and noticing the emotion, the internal affect regulation.

This example shows that phase 1 can take a long time. When our alarm systems have been consistently 'switched on' for a number of years it feels threatened and the thought of feeling safe is terrifying. It can feel like it is more dangerous to be regulated even when we understand there is no current threat and that it could benefit our relationships and daily life. Clients have often reported that being socially connected feels 'scary', 'unnatural', sometimes even 'boring' initially, as it is not familiar. However, by exploring why this might be the case, using psychoeducation as a tool to stay curious, gradually a sense of grounding and stabilisation can occur.

PHASE 2: REMEMBRANCE AND MOURNING

Remembrance and mourning can begin when the client has gained enough stability. The key principle of trauma-informed work is about learning not to re-activate the trauma responses in our body, mind, and brain. There is no clear timeframe or awareness when one is ready to move into the second phase of remembering and mourning. Within the counselling setting, it may manifest when the client is able to use the learnt skills to think about the traumatic event and notice how their body responds. If the client can regulate (even if it's uncomfortable) their emotion in the here and now using the tools that they have learnt, this perspective will allow them to challenge their old belief systems. Being able to see that they were not responsible for how someone else behaved, and that they could not have been able to stop the experience from hurting them, frees them from the guilt and from the thought, "I should have said something, I didn't, so it must have been my fault".

When an adult childhood abuse survivor realises "that without the abuser being present in their lives, they would not have been hurt or traumatised", this realisation can be transformational (Lee, 2020). The child would not have been hurt if a (bad) person had not done something to hurt them – the responsibility shifts from the victim to that person. This realisation shifts the sense of self, and the negatively associated emotions (shame, guilt, etc.) are less intense. This emotional downregulation allows them to be able to access the cognitive brain and think differently about their experiences. Clients can often experience intense grief or anger in this phase when they recognise the loss of a 'good enough' childhood, especially when they realise that they were not protected by safe adults or did not have a secure attachment.

In phase 2 the therapists can utilise their core training combined with creativity to support clients in processing their experiences. Often, using more creative interventions or metaphors can be very useful to enable clients to create a space and distance between the self that experienced the trauma and the self that is able to look upon it now as an experience. If the client does experience dissociation(s), then the parts that emerge can be worked with individually to then be able to integrate into the client's core self. Fragmented parts usually are an adaptive response to complex trauma. Internal family systems and sensorimotor psychotherapies utilise the language and skills needed to view aspects of self through a different lens (Schwartz, 2023). This can support clients to recognise the impact of what has happened to them, how they feel, and what they might need to process the ongoing impact. They may notice the changes, but sometimes can experience the emotions or physical response with more intensity than they may be able to handle. This is where the therapist needs to support the process (stop if necessary), re-establish safety and boundaries, and hold them in the present. It is here that they may also experience grief for the loss and remember the trauma.

Eye movement desensitisation regulation (EMDR) may be a useful intervention to support this phase, but it is vital that it happens once the relationship is established with the therapist and the client can stabilise and stay present. Clients can achieve similar results by using different interventions. EMDR may not work if there are more levels of trauma and other complex mental health challenges. The therapist then needs to look for other interventions that may be more suitable. Some clients will benefit from EMDR, which processes the trauma through the limbic system or in other words by connecting to the emotional sense, instead of initially accessing the cognition and thought. Thinking about the trauma and the belief system without establishing the sense of safety may not be ideal, especially in trauma-informed work or when dealing with complex trauma. This sense of safety allows the client to shift the stored implicit traumatic memories and belief systems while regulating the nervous system.

Once the clients feel that they are more regulated in their normal everyday lives, or their quality of life is different, or they feel more stable and engaged in their relationships, they may no longer want to go back and remember the traumatic event. This motivates them to stop therapy, which is their choice, and that is OK. The client may not want to explore further, or they may *choose not to*, and it is important for the therapist to respect that choice or the client's decision. Some clients may engage with phase 1 and/or phase 2, leave therapy and come back later, or may not return. But every step is closer to 'good enough' trauma-informed work.

PHASE 3: RECONNECTION

If and when a client has completed their processing, they may move to the next phase (i.e., reconnection). Some clients are very aware of their childhood traumatic experience and engaged with the therapy. An example from SF is a client with neurodiversity who, in the initial 6 to 8 months shifted effectively from phase 1 to phase 3, took a break, and came back later to continue to process other experiences. Not only was the client able to reconnect but she was able to use the skills and experience from the therapeutic sessions in her everyday life. Reconnecting is a phase where the client considers more about who they are in the world, how they relate to others, engage in decision making for themselves, make choices about how they live, and interact with others, including the therapist. For someone with complex-PTSD, the sense of social connection beyond what was needed to survive may have never happened – or happened only as and when needed. This phase empowers the client to see a new self and be able to reconnect. This is often the ending phase of the work, and the therapist may need to remind the client with some grounding skills (phase 1), as it can be scary to 'go alone' and we need to return to the tried and tested stabilisation techniques to remember "that we are okay". The client may choose to come back or dip into a set of sessions, which is more commonly seen with someone who may be neurodiverse. Especially as long durations may not be effective, they may be able to discuss, or the therapist (with the knowledge) can discuss this, as part of the initial goals or expectations. Having worked with clients who may be neurodiverse, the benefit of 20 to 30 sessions, a break, and then another bunch of sessions with a clear goal often is more effective, as the client is able not only to reconnect with themselves, but in their time reconnect with the world. Depending on the client, the therapist and client may agree on having or not having check-ins during the breaks. It is also remembering that the grounding and stabilisations techniques may have to be adapted especially when you are being flexible because of the client's experience. It is essential to remind clients to engage and keep the tools handy as they go into the reconnection and finally move out of therapy.

Witnessing a client cycle through these phases of work is a privilege. To reflect on how a client is different from when they first presented in therapy and where they are at the end can be staggering. However, the work is slow and when we are in it, it can be hard for both client and therapist to notice the small incremental changes It is vital to acknowledge the small and continued growth that clients make on this journey − to notice that the client is not as anxious sitting in their session, to recognise that they didn't respond in such an extreme way, or that they could tolerate someone noticing them or apologising for missing them. Post-traumatic growth (Sanderson, 2013) is the antidote to post-traumatic stress for everyone working in and experiencing the impact of trauma. Tracking and monitoring this with clients can mean the work is tolerated and we recognise the process we are in together.

To conclude, we use a case study to illustrate the complex journey to recovery. The client (MH) was a 48-year-old female client working with one of the authors (AW). She initially presented with extreme dissociative symptoms; she would faint and collapse whenever she was overwhelmed or perceived a threat. She had been discharged from mental health services and deemed 'too complex' for her GP to manage. She worked for a period of 2 years in weekly therapy. AW also felt overwhelmed in the work. It would be quite usual for the client to dissociate in session. She would want to talk about the most recent sexual traumas, but then not be able to manage the dysregulation that accompanied trying to tell her story. AW worked hard to explain why her brain was protecting her, but she was unwilling to attempt to regulate herself, and she wanted someone else to 'do it for me'. As time went on, AW was consistently noticing when MH's system started to react, and a routine developed within the session. There would be an arriving period where AW would create a dialogue with MH's here and now self and to some extent regulate into the room. At the end of the session AW would also allow time to come back to the space, using movement to regulate – pressing hands against the wall and feeling the power shift back into the client's body. After about 6 months the client could tolerate putting together a 'headline' timeline, with no details but an indication of what was experienced and at what age. This process took about another 6 months as it was done little by little each week. AW noticed that as time progressed the client was taking more responsibility in regulating herself. AW didn't need to intervene so quickly or so often and there were some weeks where the client stayed fully present all through the session. This was recognised and celebrated with the client. She noticed the impact of this, and her relationship needs from AW were able to be voiced. She began to be able to say what she wanted to say and know that she wouldn't be punished for having feelings. By the end of the work, whilst still significantly impacted by the traumas she had experienced, she was much more able to stay present, identify and vocalise her needs, and the relationships she had with her family were greatly improved.

On ending the work with the client, AW reflected that she was aware that the client had mostly stayed in phase 1 throughout the 2 years, dipping into phase 2 occasionally. The client was able to articulate that she was feeling safe within the relationship with AW and that had enabled her to feel empowered enough to make choices about how she was responding, to know that she was okay, to have and implement clear boundaries with those around her. AW was able to notice that it was sharing knowledge about the impact of trauma with the client in phase 1 that allowed her to feel less 'bad' and more in control of her trauma responses, which in turn enabled the client to feel able to develop a strong therapeutic alliance, or attachment to AW. It was this alliance (attachment) that carried them both through tough areas in the material to begin to live a different life. As the work ended both AW and the client could see the post-traumatic growth, and it was transformational for both.

CELEBRATION OF POST-TRAUMATIC GROWTH

Thinking about the journey of recovery, kintsugi is the first image that comes to mind. This lovely Japanese art focuses on how to recreate a valuable piece from broken pottery, by joining them together with precious metal, making them not only more durable but also expensive. Applying this analogy to trauma, the experience of healing makes the individual not only unique as they grow to a more aware and complete self but also, they can integrate parts of themselves that experienced the trauma. This journey, though beautiful, takes a lot of effort, pain, and endurance to get through. Hence the other image that comes with trauma counselling is that of a butterfly coming out of a cocoon, which is painful, but each butterfly is beautiful and has its own unique design even if they are from the same breed or family.

One of the common myths was, "it's not easy to recover from one's past or the experience of trauma" or "one cannot change their attachment styles". But today, there is a lot of research that has evidenced recovery across the spectrum. In both of our (SF and AW) clinical experience, we have seen individuals shift from their past and recover. The past does bring in a unique experience that is key to them developing their journey, but the change is inevitable. Although one cannot change their attachment styles from their childhood, being aware of the patterns and being able to make new secure attachments in their adult self and within their relationships can shift the old patterns and this has been seen with clients in our practice.

An example is a neurodiverse client who was 19 years old when she started engaging in trauma-informed therapy with SF. She had had sessions with other counsellors from the age of 16 years and had noticed the PTSD symptoms from her childhood sexual abuse come up. In 6 to 9 months of working within a trauma-informed process, she was able to be aware and understand how to use the tools and skills learnt in the sessions, applying it outside in her everyday life. It was not that she did not experience any further traumatic symptoms, but when faced with an unwanted event, she was able to choose her response and look back at her life while also being able to regulate and experience her emotion. Often the need to not experience the grief or shame can be very exhausting but being able to release it safely in therapy disperses the emotion rather than suppresses it. This was a rare example, where even though the client has a lot more journey to complete, within a short period she was able to engage in all three phases for some of her experience, but she is still in the process of recovery.

While the above was a positive shift, some clients may not be able to see such a growth, but any shift is one step closer to recovery. In another example, AW's client who worked in a trauma-informed process for over 2 years, was only ever able to engage in phase 1. Whilst this was frustrating for them, the client's day-to-day life greatly improved. So, although they still experienced significant trauma and symptoms when faced with a trigger, they were able to respond and regulate much more quickly while maintaining their relationships. This was so significant because prior to her therapy, her relationships would break down consistently and repeatedly. She learnt how to repair relationships that were important to her.

In this path, often the expectation of the individual, family, and the counsellor are to see a massive tangible shift. But it is all those small changes that occur, including being able to say no, decide to or be able to do something that means a lot for that individual, or even just self-soothing, that makes a difference. Every slight change or shift is a cause for celebration and is a victory for the individual. In the therapeutic sense, celebrating success can happen from the very beginning; noticing and recognising small changes in regulation, accountability, and belief systems throughout the work supports emotional and neural regulation, leading to change. It is in the ending that reflection on the whole process can enable both the client and the therapist to acknowledge how far they have come together, celebrating a successful relationship and acknowledging that this relational journey has allowed the healing to happen.

NOTE

1 Led by Alison Woodward, Gerry Jones, and Shanti Farrington working collaboratively with local counsellors and therapists to evidence trauma-informed practices used in clinical context within Dorset and local areas.

REFERENCES

Ainsworth, M. D. S. (1982). Attachment: Retrospect and prospect. In C. M. Parkes & J. Stevenson-Hinde (Eds.), *The place of attachment in human behavior* (pp. 3–30). Basic Books.

Ainsworth, M. D. S. (1989). Attachments beyond infancy. *American Psychologist*, 44, 709–716.

Ainsworth, M. D. S., Blehar, M. C., Waters, E., & Wall, S. (1978). *Patterns of attachment: A psychological study of the strange situation*. Erlbaum.

Alexander, J. C., Eyerman, R., Giesen, B., Smelser, N. J., & Sztompka, P. (2004). *Cultural trauma and collective identity*. University of California Press.

American Psychiatric Association. (2013). *Diagnostic and statistical manual of mental disorders* (5th ed.). American Psychiatric Association.

American Psychological Association. (2023). https://www.apa.org/topics/trauma#:~:text=Trauma%20is%20an%20emotional%20response,symptoms%20like%20headaches%20or%20nausea.

Beebe, B. (2010). Mother – infant research informs mother – infant treatment. *Clinical Social Work Journal*, 38, 17–36.

Belenky, G. (Ed.). (1987). *Contemporary studies in combat psychiatry* (p. 4). Greenwood Press.

Berne, E. (1961). *Transactional analysis in psychotherapy*. Grove Press.

Berne, E. (1972). *What do you say after you say Hello? The psychology of human behaviour*. Grove Press.

Boon, S., Steele, K., & Van Der Hart, O. (2011). *Coping with trauma-related dissociation: Skills training for patients and therapists*. WW Norton & Company.

Bowlby, J. (1969). Disruption of affectional bonds and its effects on behaviour. *Canada's Mental Health Supplement*, 59, 12.

Bowlby, J. (1973). *Attachment and loss: Vol. 2: Separation: Anxiety and anger*. Basic Books.

Bowlby, J. (1980). *Attachment and loss: Vol. 3: Sadness and depression*. Basic Books.

Bowlby, J. (1982). *Attachment and loss: Vol. 1: Attachment* (2nd ed.). Basic Books.

Cannon, W. B. (1929). *Bodily changes in pain, hunger, fear and rage: An account of recent researches into the function of emotional excitement.* D. Appleton.

Cohen, S., & Wills, T. A. (1985). Stress, social support, and the buffering hypothesis. *Psychological Bulletin, 98,* 310–357.

Erikson, E. H. (1994). *Identity and the life cycle.* WW Norton & Company.

Ernst, F. H. (1971). The OK corral: The grid for get-on-with. *Transactional Analysis Bulletin,* 1(4), 33–42.

Fisher, J. (2017). *Healing the fragmented selves of trauma survivors: Overcoming internal self-alienation.* Taylor & Francis.

Fisher, J. (2021). *Transforming the living legacy of trauma; A workbook for survivors and therapists.* PESI Publishing & Media.

Foa, E. B., Chrestman, K. R., & Gilboa-Schechtman, E. (2008). *Prolonged exposure therapy for adolescents with PTSD emotional processing of traumatic experiences, therapist guide.* Treatments That Work.

Ford, J. D., Grasso, D. J., Elhai, J. D., & Courtois, C. A. (2015). Social, cultural, and other diversity issues in the traumatic stress field. *Posttraumatic Stress Disorder,* 503.

Freud, S. (1915/1957). Repression. In J. Strachey (Ed.), *The standard edition of the complete psychological works of Sigmund Freud* (Vol. 14). Hogarth Press.

Gonzalez, A. (2018). *It's not me: Understanding complex trauma, attachment and dissociation.* ISBN 10: 8409066866ISBN 13: 9788409066865.

Harvey, M. R. (1996). An ecological view of psychological trauma and trauma recovery. *Journal of Traumatic Stress, 9,* 3–23.

Herman, J. (1992). *Trauma and Recovery: The aftermath of violence – from domestic abuse to political terror.* Basic Books.

Hughes, D. (2018). *Building the bonds of attachment: Awakening love in deeply traumatized children* (3rd ed.) Rowman & Littlefield.

Huttenlocher, P. R. (1984). Synapse elimination and plasticity in developing human cerebral cortex. *American Journal of Mental Deficiency, 88*(5), 488–496.

Lee, D. (2020). www.youtube.com/watch?v=dy4zHswm_eU

Lee, D., & James, S. (2012). *The compassionate mind approach to recovering from trauma: Using compassion focused therapy.* Hachette UK.

Lely, J. C., Smid, G. E., Jongedijk, R. A., Knipscheer, J. W., & Kleber, R. J. (2019). The effectiveness of narrative exposure therapy: A review, meta-analysis and meta-regression analysis. *European Journal of Psychotraumatology, 10*(1), 1550344.

Levine, P. A. (1997). *Waking the tiger: Healing trauma: The innate capacity to transform overwhelming experiences.* North Atlantic Books.

Levine, P. A. (2010). *Healing trauma: A pioneering program for restoring the wisdom of your body.* ReadHowYouWant. Com

Levine, P. A. (2015). *Trauma and memory: Brain and body in a search for the living past: A practical guide for understanding and working with traumatic memory.* North Atlantic Books.

Levy, K. N., Ellison, W., Scott, L. et al. (2011). Attachment style. *Journal of Clinical Psychology, 67*(2), 193–203.

Levy, K. N., & Kelly, K. M. (2009). Using interviews to assess adult attachment. In J. H. Obegi & E. Berant (Eds.), *Attachment theory and research in clinical work with adults* (pp. 121–152). The Guilford Press.

MacLean, P. D. (1990). *The triune brain in evolution: Role in paleocerebral functions.* Springer Science & Business Media.

McLean, C. P., & Foa, E. B. (2011). Prolonged exposure therapy for post-traumatic stress disorder: A review of evidence and dissemination. *Expert Review of Neurotherapeutics, 11*(8), 1151–1163.

Myers, C. M. (1915). Contributions to the study of shell shock. *Lancet, 13,* 316–320.

Niederland, W. G. (1968). Clinical observations on the "survivor syndrome". *The International Journal of Psychoanalysis, 49*(2–3), 313–315.

Obegi, J. H., & Berant, E. (Eds.). (2009). *Attachment theory and research in clinical work with adults.* The Guilford Press.

Ogden, P., Minton, K., & Pain, C. (2006). *Trauma and the body: A sensorimotor approach to psychotherapy.* W. W. Norton & Company.

Orcutt, C. (2012). *Trauma in personality disorder: A clinician's handbook.* AuthorHouse

Palmer, S. (2001). The multimodal approach. *Multicultural Counselling: A Reader, 57.*

Papez, J. W. (1937). A proposed mechanism of emotion. *Archives of Neurology & Psychiatry, 38,* 725–743.

Poole, N., & Greave, L. (2012). *Becoming trauma informed.* Centre for Addiction and Mental Health (CAMH).

Porges, S. W. (2011). *The polyvagal theory: Neurophysiological foundations of emotions, attachment, communication, and self-regulation.* W.W. Norton & Co.

Porges, S. W. (2017). *The pocket guide to the polyvagal theory: The transformative power of feeling safe.* WW Norton & Co.

Raskin, N. J., & Rogers, C. R. (2005). Person-centered therapy. In R. J. Corsini & D. Wedding (Eds.), *Current psychotherapies* (7th ed., instr. ed., pp. 130–165). Thomson Brooks/Cole Publishing Co.

Sam, D. L., & Berry, J. W. (2006). *The Cambridge handbook of acculturation psychology.* Cambridge University Press.

Sanderson, C. (2013). *Counselling skills for working with trauma: Healing from child sexual abuse, sexual violence and domestic abuse.* Jessica Kingsley Publishers.

Schore, A. N. (2003). *Affect dysregulation and disorders of the self.* W. W. Norton & Co.

Schwartz, R. C. (2023). *Introduction to the internal family systems model.* Sounds True.

Siegel, D. J. (1999). *The developing mind: Toward a neurobiology of interpersonal experience*. Guildford Press.

Sheen, K., Slade, P., & Spiby, H. (2014). An integrative review of the impact of indirect trauma exposure in health professionals and potential issues of salience for midwives. *Journal of Advanced Nursing*, 70(4), 729–743.

Smith, J., & Gillon, E. (2021). Therapists' experiences of providing online counselling: A qualitative study. *Counselling and Psychotherapy Research*, 21(3), 545–554.

Solomon, M. (2011, March). The trauma that has no name: Early attachment issues. In Presentation at the psychotherapy networker conference, Washington DC.

Sourander, A. (1998). Behavior problems and traumatic events of unaccompanied refugee minors. *Child Abuse & Neglect Journal*, 22, 719–727

Steele, K., Boon, S., & van der Hart, O. (2016). *Treating trauma-related dissociation: A practical, integrative approach* (Norton Series on Interpersonal Neurobiology). W. W. Norton & Company.

Stoll, J., Müller, J. A., & Trachsel, M. (2020). Ethical issues in online psychotherapy: A narrative review. *Frontiers in Psychiatry*, 10, 993.

Suarez, E., & Gadalla, T. M. (2010). Stop blaming the victim: A meta-analysis on rape myths. *Journal of Interpersonal Violence*, 25(11).

Tau, G. Z., & Peterson, B. S. (2010). Normal development of brain circuits. *Neuropsychopharmacology*, 35(1), 147–168

Taylor, S. E. (2009). *Health psychology*. McGraw-Hill.

Uhernik, J. A. (2016). *Using neuroscience in trauma therapy: Creative and compassionate counseling*. Routledge.

UK Trauma Council. (2023). www.gov.uk/government/publications/working-definition-of-trauma-informed-practice/working-definition-of-trauma-informed-practice

Van Der Kolk., B. (2014). *The body keeps the score: Mind, brain and body in the transformation of trauma*. Viking Press.

Wiese, E. B. P. (2010). Culture and migration: Psychological trauma in children and adolescents. *Traumatology*, 16(4), 142–152.

Wiese, E. B. P. (or Batista Pinto, E.), & Burhorst, I. (2007). Trans- cultural psychiatry: A mental health program for asylum-seeking and refugee children and adolescents in the Netherlands. *Transcultural Psychiatry*, 44, 596–613.

Winfrey, O., & Perry, B. (2021). *What happened to you? Conversations on trauma, resilience, and healing*. Boxtree.

Wolynn, M. (2017). *It didn't start with you: How inherited family trauma shapes who we are and how to end the cycle*. Penguin.

Woodward, A. (2017). *Certified transactional analyst dissertation*. Metanoia Institute.

World Health Organisation. (2018). *ICD-11 for mortality and morbidity statistics*. https://pesquisa.bvsalud.org/portal/resource/pt/lis-46337

APPENDIX

Table 1 Exercises to support coping with some common trauma symptoms

Symptoms	Exercise
	Breathing techniques are often a good place to start practicing grounding techniques as they don't require any equipment and can be done anywhere (most people wouldn't notice that you are doing it, so they are perfect to use on public transport, in the waiting room at the GP surgery, or in your own front room). They come in various forms, and because our breath is the only aspect of our autonomic nervous system that we can have a sense of control over, it is the fastest way for our limbic system to know that we are safe and that we can begin to regulate and calm. Controlling our breath, particularly our out breath sends a message to our limbic system that we are okay, which in turn means the production of cortisol and adrenalin reduces, helping regulate and slow our heart rate and calm our entire system.
Panic attacks	Focus: Slowing breathing down and recognising the here and now situation. Activity: Look around you and find a steady focus point in your environment or hold on to something physical like a stone or a fidget toy or anything that may be comforting to you. Now slowly breath in through your nose and out through your mouth, paying particular attention to your outbreath, making it longer than your inbreath. You can use counting to do this or see if you can lengthen your breath each time you take one, so the next breath lasts longer than the previous one.

(Continued)

Table 1 (Continued)

Symptoms	Exercise
	If you are struggling with this, then place your hands on your diaphragm and press in slightly to feel the body sensation to your breath and do this initially for a few minutes and gradually increase the length of your outbreath.
	If you have thoughts racing through your head like "I'm going to die" or "I can't breathe" notice them and find a gentle challenge for your thoughts. An example might be to tell yourself, "*I can breathe, it's feeling hard at the moment but I am breathing, my body will breathe for me, I am okay*", or you could say, "*I know it feels like I'm going to die, but I'm not, I've done this before, I know it will pass and I will be okay*".
	Once the panic has passed find a calm, quiet space and continue your deep breathing. Be kind to yourself and recognise that you have survived the panic, you are alive. Be curious about what your trigger was. What might help you in the future if the same situation arose again?
Anxiety	Focus: Reducing body sensations by using breath and mindfulness.
	Activity: To reduce the physical symptoms of anxiety a different type of breathing activity might be quite helpful. This is sometimes called the 7-11 (or 3-5) breathing technique, as we use counting to time our breathing, or you could name it yourself so that it means something to you; something like 'calm breathing' or 'breathing out' could work.
	Find yourself a comfortable space where you feel safe. Then bring your attention to your breath. You are going to focus on your outbreath more during this exercise to activate your parasympathetic nervous system, and therefore you want the outbreath to be longer than your inbreath. As you breathe in using all of your diaphragm, breathing deep into your tummy, count slowly to 7 by using the technique 1-and-2-and-3-and-4, etc., and then when your lungs are as full as they can be, start to breathe out slowly for a count to 11, using the same slow counting technique. Repeat this breathing cycle for six cycles initially (increase if you feel comfortable) and then return to normal breathing.
	Notice how you were feeling before and afterwards. What is the difference? Reflect upon what you liked and didn't like about the exercise.

Symptoms	Exercise
	Breathing in and out for this long can be a challenge to start with so, if you find this difficult, you can reduce the counts and start with an inbreath for a count of 3 and an outbreath for a count of 5. Once you have mastered this, gradually increase the length of time you are breathing to enhance the effectiveness.

An alternative exercise that you can use is called box breathing. The same principle applies in that you are aiming to have slow regulated in and out breathes but the technique is slightly different here. Imagine you can see a square shape in front of you like this:

Lift your preferred hand up in front of your face and start at the top left corner, using your finger to trace the shape of the imaginary box. Move your finger along the first horizontal line across the top whilst breathing in for a count of 4, then hold your breath and move your hand down the right-hand vertical edge, again counting to 4. Then move your hand to the left along the bottom horizontal line whilst breathing out and counting to 4, and then for the final vertical line, move your hand up so you get back to where you started whilst holding your breath again for a count of 4. Repeat 4 or 5 times. As in the previous exercise the counts should be slow using the technique 1-and-2-and-3-and-4. You can develop your own little rhythm and pattern, you could say, "in, 2, 3, 4 – hold, 2, 3, 4 – out, 2, 3, 4 and hold 2, 3, 4".

It is important to remember that if these breathing exercises feel too invasive or tricky some people, especially with neurodiverse conditions, may find drawing or fidgeting very relaxing instead. Experiment and use a method that helps you regulate your nervous system and helps you feel calmer.

(Continued)

Table 1 (Continued)

Symptoms	Exercise
Sleep disturbances	Focus: To improve restorative sleep and recharge the mind and body. Activity: Creating a sleep routing and good sleep hygiene. We know sleep can often feel difficult in the aftermath of trauma. These are some hints and tips to help you consider what might be useful to regulate your sleep. Initially it is important for you to think about your current sleep routine. Do you have a regular bedtime or do you avoid going to bed? Map out your current habits and then think about the points below to enable you to have a better sleep hygiene routine.

1. Try to maintain a regular time to go to bed (sleep) and wake (get up). This will help to regulate your body clock. Even if you cannot fall asleep, try to be in bed around the same time each night and avoid using phones or reading in bed. Also try to notice how close to bedtime you are watching TV and think about whether you might want to turn off the TV a couple of hours before your bedtime.

2. Create a relaxing environment in your bedroom so that you feel safe and calm when you are in your room and try to keep it free from clutter, noise, and bright light. Some things you can do to help with this is to find relaxing music that you enjoy or change a light bulb so that the light is warmer in your room, having soft furnishings like blankets and pillows that you feel are comfy and perhaps a particular scent that will help you calm down and get ready for sleep (lavender is often good for this).

3. Think about your caffeine intake and/or any energy drinks during the day and try to reduce your intake towards bedtime. Some individuals find it difficult to sleep if they have caffeinated drinks after 4:00 pm. You can swap out caffeine for decaf or consider herbal tea or hot chocolate or water.

4. Think about your current napping habits and modify them if you think they mean that you are not tired by bedtime. Sometimes, napping during the day will help you cope with fatigue so it is okay to take a nap. However, if you have long naps and feel absolutely shattered, it is important you try to regulate your naps and have a longer sleep cycle at night.

Symptoms	Exercise
	5. As part of your routine, think of any activities that would help you wind down to signal to your body that you are getting ready for bed. This can include things like having a warm drink (milk or herbal tea), writing a to-do list for the next day so that you are not thinking about any stressors whilst in bed, reading a book (not using a phone to do this due to the blue light omitted), and/or listening to a short body scan or meditation in bed.
	Notice the changes that these aspects might make to your sleep patterns. Keeping a sleep diary can really help this and make you feel like you are in control of your sleep.
Dissociative/ disconnected experiences	Focus: To bring you back into the present and feel connected to the world and your surroundings.
	Activity: Orientation to your environment – getting connected.
	When we dissociate or disconnect, we know that our survival system has been activated. When this happens we are already in our flop response and so our parasympathetic system is too active – we have downregulated so much we are no longer present, so the purpose of this activity is to bring your body and mind back to the present by orientating yourself into the here and now. This exercise is called the five senses approach. You can do this for yourself, or you can get someone you trust to do it with you.
	To use your senses, start with SIGHT, looking around your environment and find five separate things you can see and name and notice something about each. For example: the yellow clock, the white mug, the black table, the green cactus, the blue dream catcher.
	Then move on to your sense of TOUCH. Find four things you can touch and name them: the soft sweater; the hard floor; the warm blanket; and the smooth stone.
	Then moving onto your sense of HEARING, notice three things you can hear and think something about it, for example, the birds chirping, the clock ticking, the washing machine going.

(Continued)

Table 1 (Continued)

Symptoms	Exercise
	Then move to your sense of SMELL. Notice two things you can smell, for example, the perfume you're wearing, the smell of cut grass.
	Finally, move to your sense of TASTE. Notice one thing you can taste, for example, the last thing you ate or drank, or you can eat a raisin or fruit and taste it.
	As you come to the end of the exercise notice how your body feels, notice your feet beneath you, and run through the following questions in your mind:
	- What day is it today?
	- What time of day is it?
	- What am I doing next, where do I need to be?
	- How am I feeling right now? Am I connected to my body?
	If you don't feel connected, place your arms around yourself (like you are giving yourself and hug) and squeeze your arms gently, moving up and down your arms so that you are giving yourself a sense of where your body is. You can stand up and shake your arms and legs or pat your legs with your hands to make a noise. All these things help your mind and body reconnect.
General sense of grounding	Focus: Other techniques that can help you feel grounded and present.
	Activity: Visualisation and body scans.
	If you find the activities outlined above hard then give either of these options a try too. They are both designed to bring mindful awareness to your here and now presence and often there are widely available apps or websites you can use to guide you.
	Visualisation:
	Often visualisation techniques help individuals calm down and regulate their nerves by using an internal imagined safe or calm space to support your nervous system to relax. Common spaces are to create a beach, or a quiet nook in a forest, or wrapped up warm in front of the fire. You can find good resources for guided visualisations online on YouTube or other websites.[1]

Symptoms	Exercise
	Body scan or meditation:
	Similar to the visualisation techniques, there are number of body scan techniques or videos you can find online. The work by Jon Kabat Zinn is what I (SF) often use, but you can find what suits you and/or your journey. You can start with a few short meditations or body scans lasting from 3 to 5 minutes and build for practice up to 30 or 45 minutes over time. Unlike visualisations, body scans tend to focus on the sensations in the body and what you notice in real time, rather than creating an imagined space (as in visualisations).
Nightmares	Focus: To reduce nightmare occurrence and increase sleep depth.
	Activity: Dream completion technique – practice every night before sleep to encourage a different ending (safe and resolved) to your nightmares.
	We are directing you to an external resource here as we have seen how beneficial it is for our clients. Justin Havens, an EMDR therapist, has developed a very effective dream completion technique to support veterans who experienced nightmares following combat. It is a technique that allows you to take control of the ending of your nightmare, allowing your brain to process the fear in a different way.
	The link is provided here; follow the 6-minute video and then consider how you can implement the technique into your sleep routine.
	https://www.youtube.com/watch?v=lv38dzpcxfA

Table 2 The characteristics of each attachment style

Attachment Style	Traits from Parenting Style	Traits in the Child	Traits in the Adult
Secure	Present: – Attentive – Responsive – Recognises when things have gone wrong and repairs with the child – Supports regulation	Present: – Will explore, ask questions, and return to caregiver for reassurance – Can relate to others well – Uses play to explore – Sense of security in the world and confidence	Present: – Feel warmly towards ourselves – Accept flaws and mistakes – Confident they will have support when needed – Can self-soothe and ask for help
Insecure ambivalent	Inconsistent or intrusive: – Inconsistent in their response, sometimes loving, sometimes punishing – Confusing messages – High parental anxiety – Smothering, unable to let the child move away, keeping them close	Preoccupied: – Child will seek care, want closeness but it will not soothe them – They may have angry outbursts and find it hard to regulate – They look to anyone else to help them regulate	There and then gone: – Erratic with their emotions and may overreact – May love to argue but never reach a resolution – Seeks care from others but never feels 'good enough' to accept the care, often rejecting it – Cannot articulate their needs or soothe themselves – looking to the other all the time

Insecure avoidant	Unavailable or rejecting	Independent and disconnected	Self-reliant and distant
	– Consistent in care but absent – Emotionally unavailable or punishing – Lack of physical contact and emotional intelligence – Shut down	– Prefers to play on own – Doesn't confide with adults – Appears independent but disconnected from feelings – Doesn't want or seek physical connection	– Decides it is fruitless to rely upon others to meet needs – Physically and emotionally distant in relationships – Can appear self-centred and unresponsive to other's needs – Hard to recognise they have needs
Disorganised	Abusive: – Neglectful – Abusive and unpredictable – Addiction within family – Lack of boundaries or care – Chaotic	Fearful of relationships: – Trapped between seeking closeness and pulling away from feelings of terror – Disorientated and cannot regulate internally – Learning is disrupted – Cannot accept self and believes they are 'bad'	Fearful of relationships: – Cannot accept self – Disorganised and disorientated – Cannot give love and is unresponsive to other's needs – May not read social cues and experience extreme emotional problems

DSM-V CRITERIA FOR PTSD DIAGNOSIS

* Re-experiencing: covers having involuntary and uncontrolled memories of the traumatic event, recurrent dreams or nightmares related to it, flashbacks or other intense or prolonged psychological distress.
* Avoidance: covers experiencing distressing memories, thoughts, feelings, or external reminders of the event.
* Negative cognitions and mood: can represent a range of feelings that represent a distorted sense of blame of self or others, withdrawal from others or a markedly diminished interest in activities, and an inability to remember key aspects of the event (which is often terrifying and frustrating in itself).
* Arousal: can be recognised by aggressive, reckless, or self-destructive behaviours, sleep disturbances, hyper- or hypo-vigilance or other related problems.

For a diagnosis to be made the person must have had exposure to actual or threatened death, serious injury, or sexual violence in one (or more) of the following ways:

(i)   Directly experiencing
(ii) Witnessing
(iii) Learning of an event that has happened to a close family member or friend
(iv) Experiencing repeated exposure to adverse details of trauma via necessary work (e.g., first responders)

NOTE

1   You may find access to some of our resources on our website (www.thetipsuk. org).

Printed in the United States
by Baker & Taylor Publisher Services

2006